A Pocket Guide to

Nature
on O'ahu

Text and Photographs by
Michael Walther

Mutual Publishing

ISBN: 978-1939487-45-2
Library of Congress Control Number:
2014958944
All photography © Michael Walther,
unless otherwise credited
Cover design by Leo Gonzalez
Design by Courtney Tomasu

First Printing, March 2015
Second Printing, January 2017
Third Printing, June 2018
Fourth Printing, November 2018
Fifth Printing, March 2020
Sixth Printing, October 2021
Seventh Printing, September 2022

Mutual Publishing, LLC
1215 Center Street, Suite 210
Honolulu, Hawai'i 96816
Ph: 808-732-1709 / Fax: 808-734-4094
Email: info@mutualpublishing.com
www.mutualpublishing.com

Printed in China

Contents

Preface

I have owned and operated Oʻahu Nature Tours since 1995 and have conducted thousands of ecotours on this beautiful island. In order to become the absolute best "nature guide" I could be, I augmented my degree in cultural anthropology and lifelong interest in nature by eagerly studying hundreds of books, articles, and scientific papers that covered the entire spectrum of subjects that comprise Hawaiian natural history. I absorbed all the geological, geographical, meteorological, archaeological, botanical, ethnobotanical, ornithological, volcanological, and historical information about Hawaiʻi I could find. Our business motto is "Conservation through Education," and many of my guests on tour have asked me if I am a college professor. I always say no, but I tell them that being a nature guide is like being a teacher, and the beaches, mountains, and trails we visit are my classrooms.

When Mutual Publishing Company in Honolulu asked me to write this *Pocket Guide to Nature on Oʻahu,* I was honored and felt well prepared for the project. In accepting their offer, I looked forward to doing further research in all the areas I have mentioned above in order to be current with recent discoveries that related to Hawaiian natural history. Scientists in the last few years have made some amazing discoveries that have changed some long-held beliefs. Some of these include Oʻahu being composed of three volcanoes, not two; the ancestor of the Hawaiian honeycreepers is a Common Rosefinch from Asia, not a finch from North America; and the arrival of the first Polynesians in Hawaiʻi happened around AD 1,000, not as early as AD 400 as previously thought. Undoubtedly, more of the facts and truths about Hawai'i accepted today will be revised by new discoveries in the future.

O'ahu is inhabited by more than a million people every day when you include visitors and military personnel. The island has large urban areas with busy freeways, noisy industrial areas, and crowded tourist resorts. Many residents and visitors to Honolulu are overwhelmed by the numerous skyscrapers, the hustle-bustle, congested streets, and constant noise, and they long to escape the concrete jungle and find places where they can reconnect with nature. In these remaining sanctuaries, they can enjoy peace and quiet, serenity, magnificence, and timeless beauty.

My hope for this guide is that it serves as a means to educate about the island's natural history, the biological uniqueness of its flora and fauna, and its regrettable ecological past, and that it helps you find areas left on O'ahu where you can enjoy nature. Perhaps when you see one of the beautiful honeycreepers, a majestic koa tree, a colorful Hawaiian tree snail, or a ancient lobelia, spectacular products of millions of years of evolution, you will be inspired and filled with a sense of responsibility to assist these vulnerable beings that share our island home. Everyone should value what is left of O'ahu's natural heritage and work to save the native species and wild places that remain.

Michael Walther
Waikīkī, Hawai'i
January 2015

Acknowledgments

I give special thanks to my wife Cecilia for her love, friendship, continuous great advice, and support and for helping me build O'ahu Nature Tours into a successful company. Her tireless efforts organizing, operating, managing, and staffing our ecotour business have enabled me to pursue photographing Hawai'i's birds and writing my books about nature in Hawai'i.

I thank my parents for choosing to live near the Everglades in Florida and in a semirural suburb of Los Angeles. It was at these special places that I developed a love and appreciation for nature. I thank my brother Mark for his great generosity and for his excellent help in founding O'ahu Nature Tours and for keeping it going during the difficult early years.

I would like to thank Bennett Hymer, Jane Gillespie, and Courtney Tomasu at Mutual Publishing for the opportunity to write this book and for their excellent assistance with its production. I thank my professors at the University of California at Santa Barbara for the many great courses they provided, including Island Biology, American Environmental History, and Physical Anthropology. My interest in Hawaiian natural history developed from the lecturers in these classes and the papers I wrote for them. Thanks to H. Douglas Pratt, whose exceptional paintings of Hawaiian honeycreepers inspired me to move to Hawai'i in 1995.

My knowledge of nature in Hawai'i is only possible because of all the talented authors, explorers, teachers, and researchers who have conducted numerous surveys, field studies, observations, and experiments and have written the scientific papers, journal articles, websites, and books that together make up the scientific database for Hawaiian natural history that everyone has access to.

My thanks to every scientist, researcher, intern, manager, and field-worker who has studied, managed, or helped Hawai'i's native flora and fauna survive, along with their habitats. I particularly want to thank the geology professors at the University of Hawai'i, Michael Garcia and John Sinton, for their kindness in helping me be updated on recent geological discoveries and for the use of their excellent illustrations. Special thanks go to Clyde Imada for his excellent help with O'ahu's plant species; Julian Hume and Raymond Massey for allowing me to use their excellent paintings in my book; and to John Hoover for the use of his beautiful photographs of marine life.

Introduction

"Nature" is defined as the phenomena of the physical world collectively, including plants, animals, the landscape, and other features of the earth, as opposed to human creations. This guide is about the nature of O'ahu and will be useful because it provides information about the island's formation, geology, weather, natural disasters, and flora and fauna. It will help you plan where to go to enjoy some of the natural areas that remain on O'ahu. This book is not a comprehensive field guide but will assist you in identifying many of the most common bird and plant species. Geological dates are based on current research and are subject to future revisions.

I have selected some of the best places on the island where you can see examples of the remaining native flora and fauna. The 'Aiea Loop Trail and Mānoa Cliffs Trail provide access into remnant native forest areas in the Ko'olau Range. Kuli'ou'ou, Lanipō, Wa'ahila Ridge, Mānana, and Poamoho are also good trails to explore the wild areas on the Ko'olau volcano. Hiking trails in the Wai'anae Range are fewer, but the Keālia and Mokulē'ia trails offer limited access. It is best to go hiking in this area with a hiking club or group such as Hawai'i Trail and Mountain Club or the Sierra Club if you want to visit some of the best areas. Check their websites for hiking schedules.

O'ahu has 112 miles of coastline and this guide describes some of the best remaining natural coastal areas. Wetlands on O'ahu are limited and unfortunately, very few are open to the public at this time. Currently the best places to visit are Ka'elepulu Pond, also called Enchanted Lake, and Hāmākua Marsh. All of the bird images in this guide are of birds photographed in Hawai'i.

Creation of the Island

At the beginning of the Pliocene epoch about 5 million years ago, near the center of the North Pacific, the clear, turquoise water began to boil and churn. Incandescent steam clouds reached higher and higher into the dark blue tropical sky. As the erupting volcano finally reached the ocean's surface after slowly rising from the black depths, glowing lava began to dry and form a new island. Tremendous volumes of carbon dioxide, sulfur dioxide, and hydrogen sulfide were emitted into the surrounding atmosphere. Orange-red light radiated outward from the inferno, and repeated explosions rocked the fiery spectacle. The Ka'ena volcano eventually reached an altitude of over 3,000 feet. For the next one million years, steady winds, powerful waves, and frequent rains eroded the mountain. In addition to erosion, its tremendous weight and rising sea levels caused the new island to eventually subside below the surface of the ocean.

About 3.9 million years ago, a second volcano emerged on the flank of the Ka'ena volcano. For 39,000 centuries, molten lava poured forth from numerous eruptions inside the caldera and on the sides of the growing mountain until it eventually attained a height in excess of 9,000 feet.[1] This tumultuous event took place about the same time as the extinct hominid *Australopithecus anamensis* roamed the plains of East Africa. This volcano was Wai'anae, which means "water of the mullet fish." [2] Like all of the Hawaiian Islands, it was created above the Hawai'i hot spot, a stationary plume of lava that rises from 900 miles below the surface and has remained, more or less, in the same spot for 100 million years. [3] There is considerable debate

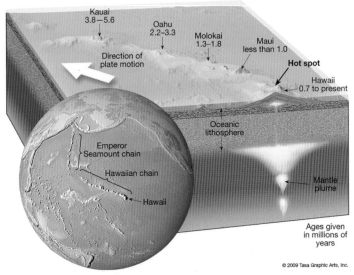

Hawaiian Hotspot.

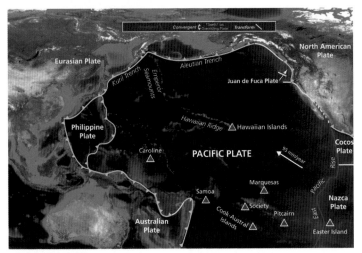

Pacific region tectonic plates.

and new research being conducted regarding the depth, location, and mechanics of this hot spot.

Every year the volcanic island is slowly dragged away from the hot spot three to four inches northwestward, carried on the immense Pacific tectonic plate as it moves above the Earth's underlying mantle.

The Ka'ena and Wai'anae volcanoes are just two of a long chain of eighty volcanoes that stretches over 3,600 miles across the North Pacific Ocean and forms the Hawaiian Island-Emperor Seamount Chain.

The oldest existing volcano, Meiji Seamount, is estimated to be about 82 million years old. It currently is located off the east coast of the Siberian peninsula of Kamchatka and is over 6,000 feet below the surface. It was once a high island like Wai'anae but was eroded to sea level and eventually submerged. Each volcanic island has a birth, life, and death and a lifespan that can last as long as 30 million years. Like a colossal conveyor belt, the volcanoes are formed over the hot spot and then slowly carried away.

All of the volcanoes in Hawai'i are classified as shield volcanoes because they have a long, broad, flat shape that looks similar to a warrior's shield. The reason for this unusual shape is that Hawaiian volcanoes have very fluid lava flows and no mountain-destroying

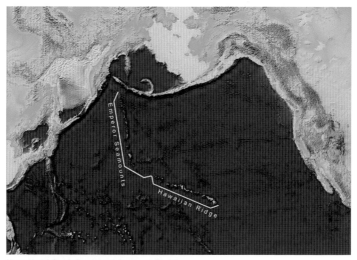

Hawaiian Island-Emperor Seamount Chain.

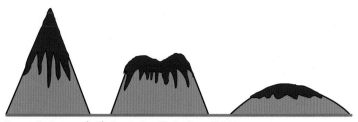
Types of volcanoes (L-R): Composite, Cinder Cone, Shield.

explosions like Krakatau or the recent devastating one at Mount St. Helens. The term "shield volcano" originates from the Skjaldbreiður volcano in Iceland. Only 10 percent of the world's volcanoes are shield volcanoes. Other familiar types of volcanoes are the strato-volcanoes, classical conical-shaped mountains such as Mount Fuji, Mount Rainier, and Mount Etna; lava domes; and cinder cones.

The Wai'anae volcano existed for approximately 1.2 million years before the Ko'olau (meaning "windward") volcano emerged from the sea about 2.7 million years ago and began to grow close to the southern edge of the Wai'anae volcano. Successive layers of very fluid molten lava eventually created a mountain over 7,000 feet high. Flows from the younger volcano gradually created a saddle, joining the two volcanoes. This area today is called the Leilehua Plateau. Once these three ancient volcanoes merged, the island of O'ahu was formed. The nicely shaped new island went through a cataclysmic event, several major disfiguring processes, and 2 million years or more of erosion, all of which contributed to its present-day rugged appearance.

One of the largest landslides in Earth's history occurred about a million years ago on O'ahu when the northeast flank of the 35-mile-long Ko'olau volcano collapsed and violently avalanched into the sea. A gigantic tsunami, esti-

Kure Atoll.

mated to be at least 300 feet high, was generated that crashed into the islands of Moloka'i and Lāna'i. The debris field, which includes several enormous blocks the size of Manhattan Island, extends 125 miles into the deep Pacific Ocean. One-third of the volcano was gone. [4]

The Nu'uanu Pali is the remaining edge of the giant Ko'olau caldera. Multiple landslides and other destructive events removed one-half of the Wai'anae volcano. The debris field lying underwater west of the mountain range is the largest in Hawai'i.

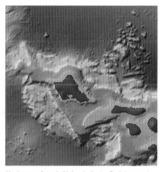

Nu'uanu landslide debris field northeast of O'ahu.

The Nu'uanu Pali is the remaining edge of the giant Ko'olau caldera.

Raised reef at Ka'ena.

Fourteen shorelines above current sea level and five submarine shelves have been documented on and around O'ahu. A combination of sea level changes due to the Earth's glacial periods and submergence of O'ahu because of its tremendous weight have created the different shorelines during the last 5 million years. Evidence for the shoreline being higher than today's level can be seen in the raised coral reefs at Ka'ena Point (80 to 100+ feet above current sea level), on the 'Ewa plain (110+ feet), and at Lā'ie (80+ feet). The submarine shorelines, one of which is Lualualei, are between 1,200 and 1,800 feet underwater and represent lower sea levels in the ancient past. The fluctuating sea levels over time have helped to sculpt the current landscapes of O'ahu. [5]

By far the most recognizable features caused by past events and processes that shaped O'ahu are those included in the Honolulu Volcanic Series.

Famous landmarks, including Le'ahi or Diamond Head Crater, Pūowaina or Punchbowl Crater, Hanauma Bay, Kohelepelepe or Koko Crater, Kuamo'okane or Koko Head, Salt Lake, and the miniature Kaimukī shield volcano plus thirty-three other tuff cones, cinder cones, and lava flows were created between 30,000 and 800,000 years ago, when the Ko'olau volcano came back to life after being

Mānoa Valley, an amphitheater-shaped valley in Honolulu.

Leʻahi or Diamond Head Crater.

dormant for almost a million years. The reason for this rejuvenation stage is not fully known or agreed upon, and the dates of all geological events on O'ahu are subject to change with new discoveries still being made.[6]

Ever since the trio of volcanoes that formed O'ahu emerged from the sea, powerful erosional forces have worked against them. The effects of constant pounding surf, strong winds, and abundant rainfall all combined to weather the enormous mountains. Huge amphi-

Kohelepelepe or Koko Crater.

Miniature Kaimukī shield volcano.

theater valleys, separated by steep-sided ridges, were carved into their pristine flanks. Mānoa, Pālolo, Nuʻuanu, Makua, Lualualei, Kaʻaʻawa, and Kahana were partially created by freshwater streams cutting through the ancient basalt since the first rains fell on their exposed slopes. The timeworn remnant volcanoes have been greatly dissected, and because of the severe deformation they are called ranges today.[7]

When you travel up Oʻahu's scenic windward or eastern coast you see many offshore islands and islets beginning with Kāohikai-pu, a cinder cone located close to the southern end of the Koʻolau volcano at Makapuʻu Point. Nearby is Mānana Island, a former tuff cone. Both of these and many of the other offshore islands are bird sanctuaries that are closed to the public. As you precede up the coast to the north shore, another fourteen islands can be seen. Perhaps the most famous is Mokoliʻi, also known as Chinaman's Hat, which is an eroded remnant of part of a former basaltic ridge of the Koʻolau volcano.

The ocean depths off Oʻahu increase rapidly, and at 30 miles off-shore the water is over 14,000 feet deep in some areas. Most of the land mass of Oʻahu is below the surface of the ocean. If you could

Oʻahu offshore islets.

remove all of the sea-water and stand on the deepest ocean floor, you could look up at a volcanic island 18,000 feet in height. A fringing reef surrounds most of O'ahu, with the exception of a few areas along the southeastern coast.

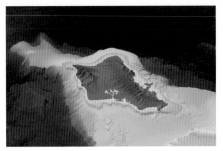

Ocean depth near O'ahu.

O'ahu is the third largest Hawaiian Island at 596.7 square miles, making it the 20th largest island in the United States. The island measures 44 miles long and 30 miles wide. The shoreline is 112 miles long, and the highest peak, Ka'ala in the Wai'anae Range, is 4,003 feet above sea level. The highest peak in the Ko'olau Range is Konahuanui.[8] O'ahu is nicknamed the "Gathering Place" and had a population estimated at 976,372 in 2012 according to the U.S. Census Bureau. This represents about 70 percent of the state's population.

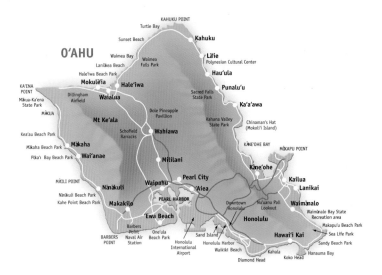

Island Weather, Rare Events, and Natural Disasters

The northernmost place on O'ahu is Kahuku Point at 21 degrees 43 minutes north latitude. Diamond Head Crater is the southernmost point at 21 degrees 16 minutes north. Located south of the Tropic of Cancer, the island has a mild climate that is relatively uniform throughout the year. Average annual high temperature in Honolulu is 84.5°F and the average low is 70.7°F. [9]

The refreshing northeast trade winds, O'ahu's primary source for rain, are the most prominent weather characteristic of the island and occur as much as 80 percent of the days in some years. There are two major seasons: the wet season, ho'oilo, from November to April, and the dry season, kau, from May to October.

The two parallel mountain ranges have a significant impact on rainfall patterns because of the orographic effect. When moisture-bearing air masses move from lower elevations on the windward side up and over the Ko'olau and Wai'anae ranges, clouds are formed and the majority of rain falls near the summits of the mountains. On the leeward side of the two ranges, dry conditions exist due to the rain shadow effect. Windward O'ahu areas have an average of 60 inches of annual rainfall, while drier areas on the leeward side, including Honolulu and Mākaha, receive less than 20 inches of rain per year. The wettest part of the Ko'olau Range averages over 240 inches of rain each year!

While the usual description of O'ahu's weather is mild or uniform, sometimes extreme weather and disasters happen. On

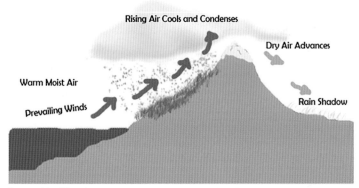

Orographic effect.

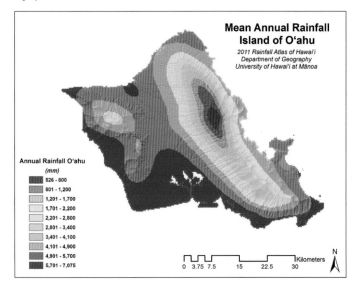

March 5 to 6, 1958, a Kona storm dropped 17.41 inches of rain in Honolulu and over 24 inches in the Koʻolau Range, the greatest daily amount ever recorded. Kona storms are a type of seasonal cyclone, with winds that come from a southwesterly direction.

The highest temperature ever recorded in Honolulu was 95°F on September 19, 1994. The record for the lowest temperature in Honolulu, 52°F, has occurred twice: February 16, 1902, and January 20, 1969. The difference between these two all-time records is only 43°F. The highest recorded temperature on O'ahu was 98°F during July 1915 at Wai'anae. Lyon Arboretum, in the back of Mānoa Valley, recorded a low temperature of 49°F in December 1983.

A 4.25-inch hailstone that dropped during a supercell thunderstorm in 2012.

On March 9, 2012, a supercell thunderstorm dropped state-record size hailstones on Kāne'ohe and Kailua during a thirty-minute hailstorm, some of which were 4.25 inches long, 2.25 inches tall, and 2 inches wide! Surprisingly, hail has been recorded on O'ahu five times since 2006. Snow pellets were reported on O'ahu at sea level on March 4, 1953, but these occurred during widespread thunderstorms and were accompanied by small hail.

O'ahu has had twenty recorded tornadoes since 1950, but none exceeded F2 in intensity. On January 28, 1971, a tornado touched down and was tracked for 2 miles. The resulting damage was over $250,000. Perhaps the most destructive tornado on O'ahu in recent times occurred on February 11, 1982, when two F2 twisters caused $500,000 damage. Some of the tornadoes that have slammed into the island started as waterspouts, but most of the these spectacular funnel clouds stay over the ocean and never impact the land.

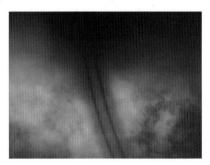

Funnel cloud in Kahuku, October 17, 2010.

Flood events happen on Oʻahu often, at least several times every decade, and many have caused serious loss of life and property. On New Year's Eve 1987, abundant rain came down all night long in the valleys of southeast Oʻahu. This was an extreme event estimated to happen only once every two hundred years. In some areas, over 20 inches of rain fell in twenty-four hours. The result was $34,000,000 in damage. The most serious flood occurred on October 30, 2004, in

Flood damage in Mānoa Valley, October 30, 2004.

Mānoa Valley. Torrential rains began to fall in the uppermost section of the valley, with amounts of 5 inches in just one hour. Mānoa Stream jumped its banks and began to wash cars away. Tons of water cascaded onto the University of Hawaiʻi campus, flooding the library and other buildings. The damage toll was $80,000,000.

The highest wind speed ever recorded in Honolulu was 80 miles per hour on the evening of November 30, 1957, when Hurricane Nina's eye passed 300 miles to the southeast. Hurricane Iwa battered Oʻahu with 30-foot waves on November 24, 1982. Six thousand homes, twenty-one hotels, and two condominiums were damaged. On September 11, 1992, the most powerful hurricane in recorded Hawaiian history, ʻIniki, a category 4 behemoth with sustained winds of 145 mph, passed close to Oʻahu and then slammed directly into Kauaʻi. Thirty thousand people were evacuated on Oʻahu. Seven people died and over $1.8 billion in property damage occurred.

Hurricane 'Iniki.

Since 1861, nineteen earthquakes have had intensities from 5.0 to 6.9 on the Richter scale on O'ahu. On February 19, 1871, a magnitude 6.8 earthquake occurred off the coast of Lāna'i. Extensive but minor damage was widespread on O'ahu. Every building at the prestigious Punahou campus needed repairs. Severe shaking and minor damage, including cracked masonry and water main breaks, happened on June 28, 1948, when the earth moved about 45 miles from downtown Honolulu. A magnitude 6.2 quake that rocked the Hāmākua coast on the island of Hawai'i on April 26, 1973, caused minor cosmetic damage on O'ahu.

The most recent large earthquake felt on O'ahu happened early Sunday morning, October 15, 2006, at 7:07 AM. The earth ruptured 18 miles below the surface off the coast of North Kona on the island of Hawai'i when the 6.7-magnitude quake hit. O'ahu, some 160 miles away, had only minor damage. High-rise buildings swayed back and forth and high-pitched grinding sounds could be heard inside the walls. The entire island had an electrical blackout that lasted fourteen hours in some areas. The state was declared a disaster area, and over $200 million in damage was recorded on the Big Island.

Surfing at Waimea Bay, north shore of Oʻahu.

Oʻahu is world famous as the capitol of surfing. Every winter, wave heights can reach 25 to 30 feet and cause little more than excitement, but in some rare years, monster surf arrives. On December 1, 1969, 50-foot waves slammed into the north shore of Oʻahu. Three intense, overlapping storms in the North Pacific helped to create the gigantic surf. Sixty homes were destroyed or badly damaged, the only road around the island was flooded, and many boats were carried away from Haleʻiwa harbor and deposited over 100 yards inland.

Tsunamis, Japanese for "great harbor waves," are the most deadly natural disasters in Hawaiʻi, and they have caused significant damage several times on Oʻahu. Twenty-seven tsunamis with flood elevations greater than 3.3 feet have hit Hawaiʻi in recorded history. Thirteen of these have reached Oʻahu and eleven caused significant damage on the island, beginning with the first event on November 7, 1837. In Honolulu, the ocean suddenly dropped 8 feet below its normal level, exposing many reefs. More than a hundred years later, Hawaiʻi's most disastrous tsunami occurred on April Fool's Day, 1946. A massive 8.1 earthquake off the coast of the Aleutian Islands in Alaska uplifted a large section of the seafloor and generated nine destructive waves that raced across the Pacific Ocean, traveling 490 miles per hour. The first wave arrived in Honolulu Harbor at 6:33 AM,

Damage to road in southeast Oʻahu from April 1, 1946 tsunami.

followed fifteen minutes later by the second wave. The height of the waves varied dramatically depending on where they hit Oʻahu. On the north side of Makapuʻu, tremendous waves over 37 feet high, the highest recorded waves to hit Oʻahu, smashed into the coast. Destructive 31-foot-high waves at the famous Hālona Blowhole rose over the sea cliffs and destroyed the coastal road. At Hanauma Bay, the waves were 14 feet, and inside Kāneʻohe Bay they were less than 1 foot.

Tornadoes, waterspouts, hailstorms, floods, hurricanes, earthquakes, and tsunamis have occurred on Oʻahu for millions of years and will continue for as long as the island exists. Except for the last thousand years or so, when people first arrived on this remote island, these powerful events caused no loss to human life or property and were part of the natural cycle. The only witnesses to these dynamic incidents were countless insects, snails, birds, bats, turtles, seals, dolphins, and whales that populated this tropical Eden.

The Arrival of Life and Evolution's Greatest Masterpieces

The flora and fauna that existed on prehuman Oʻahu can only be imagined and reconstructed from the scattered and dwindling populations that remain today, from coring samples, and from subfossils that are still being discovered. Sadly, we can only conjure up beautiful scenes from this idyllic past and paint make-believe plumages on the extinct species that no one ever described. A perfect order existed among the inhabitants and the ecosystems were in balance; overall, the appearance must have been one of sublime beauty and natural harmony. Each life zone was determined by a complex combination of location, sunlight, rainfall, elevation, temperature, and soil type.

The Hawaiian Islands are the most remote archipelago on the planet. The west coast of North America is approximately 2,300 miles to the northeast of Hilo. Japan is about 2,500 miles to the northwest of Kure Atoll and over 3,800 miles from Honolulu. Nukuhiva in the Marquesas, the nearest group of high islands, lies 2,400 miles to the southeast of Hilo. Dutch Harbor, in the Aleutians, is over 2,200 miles north of Kauaʻi. The vast expanse of ocean made it extremely difficult for many organisms to reach the distant volcanic islands.

After the molten lava flows of the newly emerged volcanic island cooled, microscopic wind-borne seeds and spores arrived. A few of these found suitable conditions, and eventually lichen and fern species began to grow on the rugged, black basalt. They had been

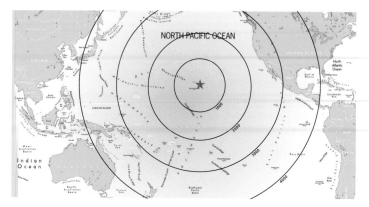

Illustration of surrounding areas showing mileage from Hawai'i.

carried high above the Earth over great distances in the jet stream, while others had their origin on the closer neighboring high islands of Kaua'i, Mokumanamana (or Necker Island), and Nihoa.

Within several years, as evidenced by recent studies of the Surtsey volcano, a variety of seabirds discovered the new island and soon began nesting colonies. Insects arrived to the remote island, along with a great variety of microorganisms. Working together, the bacteria, plants, insects, and birds coupled with the powerful forces of wind, rain, and wave erosion slowly created soil and sand.

The seeds of flowering plants arrived, most likely carried to O'ahu by shorebirds that had the propagules stuck in their feathers, in particles of dried mud on their feet, or, most commonly, inside their bodies. Some of the seeds arrived by flotation, carried to the new shoreline from distant locations. Very tiny seeds and spores were transported to the island on the persistent winds.[10] The only two mammal species that occur naturally in Hawai'i, the 'ōpe'ape'a or Hawaiian hoary bat *(Lasiurus cinereus semotus)* and the 'ilio-holo-i-ka-uaua or Hawaiian Monk seal *(Monachus schauinslandi)*, flew and swam to the new island.

For hundreds of thousands of years, the island grew in size and height, thereby creating a variety of different ecological niches that founding species adapted to by evolving into new forms. The adaptive radiations that occurred in Hawai'i are world famous, and

'Ōpe'ape'a or Hawaiian hoary bat *(Lasiurus cinereus semotus)*

'Ilio-holo-i-ka-uaua or Hawaiian Monk seal *(Monachus schauinslandi)*.

several outstanding examples occurred on O'ahu. According to the currently known distribution of Hawaiian plant species, not counting past unknown extinctions, O'ahu has 646 native plant species and subspecies.

Of these, 147 are endemic to O'ahu, meaning that they live on O'ahu and nowhere else in the world. These are priceless natural treasures that should be protected at all cost. Perhaps the most spectacular of these masterpieces of evolution are the native Hawaiian lobelias, called the "pride of our flora" by Dr. William Hillebrand, a German physician and botanist who lived in Hawai'i from 1850 to 1870. The 28 O'ahu island endemic species account for 20.1 percent of the 139 lobelia species found in Hawai'i.[11] This spectacular group

represents the most species-rich radiation of plants derived from a single colonist to be found on any of the world's islands or archipelagos. Their common ancestor arrived in the Hawaiian islands about 13 million years ago near French Frigate Shoals and Gardner Pinnacles from a yet to be determined source.[12] At that distant time, both of these were high islands. If you are fortunate enough to find and see them today struggling to survive, you are beholding a living gem. Unfortunately, 19 of the 28 (68 per-

Native Hawaiian Lobelia—*Cyanea angustifolia*.

'I'iwi, an endangered Hawaiian honeycreeper, pollinating a native lobelia.

cent) endemic O'ahu lobelia species are either endangered (16) or extinct (3).

All Hawaiian lobelias except the low-elevation Brighamia are orinthophilous, which means they are pollinated by birds who feed on the nectar produced inside the tubular-shaped flowers. The major pollinator of the lobelias, the Hawaiian honeycreepers, evolved about 5 million years ago. These "jewels of the forest" are another famous masterpiece of evolution, with fifty-six colorful species and subspecies evolving from a single ancestor believed to be an ancestral Common Rosefinch from Asia.[13, 14] This divergence is one of the best examples of adaptive radiation in birds the world has ever known. Regrettably, just like the Hawaiian lobelias they coevolved with, fifty of the fifty-six (90 percent) Hawaiian honeycreeper taxa are either endangered or extinct. On the island of O'ahu, only three of the twenty-one original honeycreeper varieties still survive! This is one of the greatest extinction events on any island in the world.

Just as the native lobelias and honeycreepers on O'ahu have been decimated, so to has another of nature's best creations in Hawai'i: the

O'ahu tree snail shells collected ca. 1933 at Wai'alae Ridge.

O'ahu tree snails in the genus *Achatinella*. These native snails, which attracted worldwide interest, evolved from a single ancestor into forty-one colorful species. Today, all of them are listed as endangered, but it is likely that only eleven species actually survive. Tens of thousands of snails were collected by hobbyists during the early 1900s.

In order to fully appreciate the incredible diversity and beauty that existed on prehuman O'ahu, it is necessary to travel back in time, use your imagination, to some unknown day over a thousand years ago on the eve of the arrival of the first Marquesan voyagers from the southeast. The island was covered in its pristine vegetation. The species found in the virgin plant communities were determined by elevation, rainfall, substrate, exposure, and topography. It is likely that a total of over eight hundred plant species and subspecies were found in the coastal lowland rain forest, mountain rain forest, dry leeward forests, and bogs and marshes. At least five species of sea turtles swam offshore and several nested on the island, most likely in great numbers. The surrounding ocean was teeming with abundant whales, seals, dolphins, fishes, and crustaceans.

The island was dominated by birds. The seabird-nesting colonies of at least twenty different species covered great areas on the offshore islands, along the coast, and in the mountains. A minimum of five flightless bird species, including ducks, geese, and rails, walked, hopped, and ran along the shores, wetlands, and in the forests. Large eagles soared in the updrafts high above the undiscovered island, and these were likely joined at times by falcons, hawks, long-legged owls, crows, and perhaps an accipiter-type hawk. Twenty species of exquisitely adapted and colorful honeycreepers flew without concern all over the island. They coexisted with several species of honeyeaters, a flycatcher, and a thrush. Many species of migratory birds would arrive on the island in the early summer, and most would stay until the following spring. The Hawaiian bats were numerous and flew at dusk to feed on the abundant insects. The lobelias and all of the native plant species were at their zenith, as were the native tree snails. Every organism was living in harmony with its environment, and a complex ecological balance existed.

O'ahu long ago was paradise on Earth. The water was clear and clean. Nothing existed on the land that was harmful to humans. There were no ants, centipedes, scorpions, fleas, or roaches. There were no snakes, lizards, poisonous frogs, or any kind of dangerous land animal.

As the next day dawned, this fragile, 5-million-year-old utopia was about to change forever.

A Fading Paradise

A large double-hulled canoe with crab-claw style sails slowly approached the inviting coast of windward Oʻahu in the early afternoon. A group of moa nalo (goose-like ducks) feeding near the beach gazed without fear at the first arriving humans. Somewhere

Extinct Oʻahu Moa Nalo *(Thambetochen xanion)*.

Polynesian junglefowl *(Gallus gallus)*.

near present-day Bellows Beach, twenty or thirty people stepped ashore.[15] After securing the vessel, they began to unload their squealing pigs *(Sus scrofa)*, loudly cackling Polynesian jungefowl *(Gallus gallus)*, and the strong-willed and curious poi dogs or 'ilio *(Canis lupus familiaris)*, which had potbellies, flattened heads, and short legs. The dogs and pigs were not easily controlled and soon began chasing the inquisitive moa-nalo. Distracted by the loud barking and frenzied action on the beach, the voyagers did not notice several 'iole or small brown Polynesian rats *(Rattus exulans)* with large round ears and pointed snouts jumping off the canoe. The first alien species had arrived in paradise.

As night fell, the rats scurried away from the new encampment and quickly began to consume the large eggs in a nearby moa-nalo nest. The dogs wandered through the beachside pandanus (hala) forest, excited by the unknown but promising scents of new food items.

'Iole or Polynesian rat *(Rattus exulans)*.

The next morning, the colonists began to look for places to begin growing the many varieties of plants they had brought with them on the long journey: kalo or taro (*Colocasia esculenta*), niu or coconut *(Cocos nucifera)*, mai'a or banana *(Musa sp.)*, and kukui or candlenut *(Aleurites moluccanus)*. An additional twenty species of nonnative plants were eventually introduced into the Hawaiian environment by the Polynesian voyagers. Some in the group fished in the near-shore waters while others began constructing basic shelters.

Within several years, the area of their new settlement began to resemble the small village from where they had come. They had successfully transplanted what was familiar to them. Native trees were cut to use for house construction, fence posts, and outrigger canoes. Areas of the pristine forest were cleared by cutting and burning so their agricultural areas could be expanded.[16] Meanwhile, the rat population exploded because they had few natural predators to keep their numbers in control, and they have very high reproduction rates. The rodents consumed the large seeds of the endemic loulu palm, causing this species to disappear from many areas within several hundred years.[17] The rats ate the eggs of the many flightless, ground-nesting birds. Some of the chickens became feral and wandered far into the coastal rain forests in search of food.

Eventually the human population on O'ahu expanded, and many areas on the island below 1,500 feet had large villages and agricultural areas. The first Europeans to go ashore on O'ahu were Captain Clerke and the crew of the HMS *Resolution*, which sailed into Waimea Bay on February 24, 1779. Clerke wrote the following account in his journal: "I stood into a Bay to the

Seeds of the native Loulu palm.

King George and the *Queen Charlotte* off Koko Head, 1786.

Westward of this point the Eastern Shore of which was far the most beautiful Country we have yet seen among these Isles, here was a fine expanse of Low Land bounteously cloath'd with Verdure, on which were *situated many large Villages and extensive plantations*; at the Water side it terminated in a fine sloping, sand Beach."[18]

Seven years later, Captain Nathaniel Portlock approached O'ahu on June 1, 1786, and passed down the south coast. He wrote the following: "...the low land and vallies being in a high state of cultivation, and crowded with plantations of taro, sweet potatoes, sugarcane etc. interspersed with a great number of coconut trees, which renders the prospect truly delightful." [19]

The combined effects of loss of habitat due to agriculture, burning, wood gathering and village building, predation by rats, dogs, and pigs, and human consumption for food caused the extinction of one-half of all known land bird species on the island. The dynamics and interactions of this massive loss of species are still being researched. [20, 21] All of the flightless taxa except one, the moho or Hawaiian Rail *(Porzana sandwichensis)*, were soon exterminated, including the fearless moa-nalo. [22, 23, 24]

Moho or Hawaiian Rail (*Porzana sandwichensis*).

It is important to remember that O'ahu's exceptional native flora and fauna had evolved in isolation for 5 million years and that humans have only been on the island about one thousand years. Imagine a 100-yard-long football field. The first three-quarters of an inch would represent the total time people have been present.

European Discovery and the Continuing Decline

The rapid demise of O'ahu's native flora and fauna accelerated even faster with the arrival of westerners. Due to the absence of large grazing animals in the Hawaiian Islands, native forest plants and trees evolved for millions of years without any need to develop thorns or chemical defenses against herbivores such as goats, sheep, or cattle.

On January 29, 1778, Captain James Cook anchored off the island of Ni'ihau. During his short visit, he introduced the first large mammals into Hawai'i's environment. The great explorer left a male and two female goats *(Capra hircus)* and a pair of large European pigs, along with pumpkin, melon, and onion seeds.

The first cattle were introduced by Captain George Vancouver on February 19, 1793. On this trip and a second trip in 1794, a total of eight females and four males were landed on the island of Hawai'i. At the same time, Vancouver introduced the first sheep, six rams and seven ewes, from California. King Kamehameha I placed a kapu (taboo) on the slaughter of cattle, and by 1830 they were numerous. The cattle, goats, sheep, and pigs were allowed to roam free, and their populations increased rapidly.[25] By the early 1800s, the grazing animals were brought to O'ahu. After fifty years, the island had 12,000 cattle, 6,500 horses, and 5,500 sheep. Many more hoofed animals had become feral and were uncountable. The cattle population on O'ahu was 15,261 in 1879, 19,625 in 1884, 27,599 in 1895, and 21,714 in 1905, according to tax records.

Widespread depletion of O'ahu's remaining dry forest and the lower to middle-altitude wet forest was caused by these destructive grazing animals, deforestation for fuel wood and building mate-

Norfolk Island pine *(Araucaria heterophylla).*

rials, ranching, the sandalwood industry, and fires. By 1870 many of the watershed areas on Oʻahu were deforested and eroding. Because the trees, shrubs, and grasses had been removed, the water no longer trickled down through the plant cover to fill up the underground aquifers, which were the source for both drinking water and for agricultural irrigation. When heavy rains occurred, the topsoil was carried away and eventually ended up in the ocean.

In 1876 the Kingdom of Hawaiʻi passed the Act for the Protection and Preservation of Woods and Forests and began efforts to control the widespread environmental destruction. In 1903, the Hawaiʻi Division of Forestry was created to protect the islands' water resources. Early forestry work on Oʻahu included establishing forest reserves, tree planting, and fencing to restrict ranch animals. From 1870 to 1961, millions of introduced trees were planted on Oʻahu as part of a massive reforestation effort. Some of these are the Norfolk Island pine *(Araucaria heterophylla)*, Molucca albizia *(Albizia falcataria)*, many eucalyptus species, Australian red cedar *(Toona ciliata)*, Silk Oak *(Grevillea robusta)*, mahogany, and tropical ash *(Fraxinus uhdei)*.

Oʻahu currently has 32,000 acres of forest reserve land, which is 9 percent of the island's total area. Some 46 percent of this area is

Oʻahu
Conservation
Areas

Koʻolau

Waiʻanae

■ Native ecosystems
☐ Degraded native ecosystems
▨ Native ecosystems no longer exist

native forest. An additional 108,700 acres of forests are not in forest reserves but are mostly included in either the Wai'anae Mountains Watershed Partnership or the Ko'olau Mountains Watershed Partnership. The lands protected by these partnerships include 76 percent of the remaining 'ōhi'a and koa forests on O'ahu.

When you hike on the lower and middle sections of the mountain ridge or valley trails on O'ahu, most of the plant and tree

Strawberry guava *(Psidium cattleianum)*.

species you see are alien species from all over the planet, many of which were introduced as part of the reforestation effort. Occasionally you might encounter a native plant or tree, but for the most part these areas are infested by strawberry guava *(Psidium cattleianum),* Christmas berry *(Schinus terebinthifolius),* lantana *(Lantana camara),* ironwood *(Casuarina equisetifolia),* fiddlewood *(Citharexylum spinosum),* octopus tree *(Schefflera actinophylla),* and hundreds of other aggressively spreading weed species. If you walk far enough onto the ridges, eventually you reach pockets of mostly native forest that have survived the ravages of the last thousand years. But even in many of these remaining sanctuaries, if you look close enough you might see the seedlings of the invading alien plant species starting to grow. They have been carried to these areas by thousands of feral pigs, introduced birds, ubiquitous rats, and the wind. Fortunately many individuals from the Oʻahu Invasive Species Committee and other environmental groups are doing what they can with limited funding to prevent further deterioration of Oʻahu's shrinking native forest.

Lantana *(Lantana camara)*.

Three additional destructive rodents were introduced into Oʻahu's environment after 1778: the Norway rat *(Rattus norvegicus)*, the black rat *(Rattus rattus)*, and the house mouse *(Mus musculus)*. Rats eat the eggs and chicks of native birds, the seeds and fruits of native plants, Hawaiian snails, native invertebrates, and

Ironwood *(Casuarina equisetifolia)*.

Asian mongoose *(Herpestes javanicus)*.

Nēnē or Hawaiian Goose *(Branta sandvicensis)*.

food items that native birds need to survive. The black rat, because of its arboreal behavior, is considered the greatest threat to native Hawaiian forest birds. They are considered a leading cause of the decline and extirpation of endemic forest birds. Rats are prolific. Female rats can have eight to twelve offspring every month as long as there is enough food, water, and shelter.

Seventy-five Asian mongoose *(Herpestes javanicus)* were brought to a Hāmākua sugarcane plantation on Hawai'i island in 1883 from Jamaica in an effort to control the rat population. The mongoose increased rapidly, and a noticeable decline of rats was recorded. In 1885 an additional 215 mongoose were imported from Jamaica and released by Joseph Marsden. He wrote the following about mongoose in a *Honolulu Advertiser* article published on December 5, 1895, which provides information contrary to the myth that mongoose never eat rats because rats are nocturnal and mongoose diurnal: "...but rats are his delight, and he pursues them relentlessly and will only turn to other things when they become scarce. In less than two years after the importation of mongoose by the writer the rats were so diminished it was and is now a rare thing to see a stick of cane that has been eaten."

Several years later, they were released on O'ahu. By 1904 it was apparent that besides eating rats, the mongoose were also preying on ground-nesting birds and their eggs, including introduced game birds, the nēnē or Hawaiian Goose (*Branta sandvicensis*), pueo or Hawaiian Owl (*Asio flammeus*), and many varieties of seabirds. Efforts to exterminate the mongoose were overwhelmingly rejected by the powerful sugarcane growers.

One of the most prolific predators of native birds on O'ahu is the house cat (*Felis catus*). In 1866, Mark Twain visited Honolulu and wrote, "I saw … tame cats, wild cats, singed cats, individual cats, groups of cats, platoons of cats, companies of cats, regiments of cats, armies of cats, multitudes of cats, millions of cats."

Pueo or Hawaiian Owl (*Asio flammeus*).

'Alae 'ula or Hawaiian Moorhen *(Gallinula chloropus)*.

Palila *(Loxioides bailleui)*.

Today, over 1,200 people are registered as feral cat colony care-givers on the island and the wild cat population is believed to be in excess of 100,000 animals. Most of these cats are infected with toxoplasmosis, which has been implicated in the deaths of native seabirds and the nēnē.

Feral cats have been observed killing the following endangered species: 'alae 'ula or Hawaiian Moorhen (*Gallinula chloropus*), Palila (*Loxioides bailleui*), 'ua'u or Hawaiian Petrel (*Pterodroma sandwichensis*), and Newell's Shearwater (*Puffinus newelli*).

The bullfrog (*Rana catesbeiana*) has also participated in the accelerated demise of O'ahu's native flora and fauna since the arrival of Europeans in 1778. They have been documented eating the chicks of all four endangered waterbird species.

Perhaps the single most important cause of the extinction and decline of native forest bird species on O'ahu was the introduction of southern house mosquitoes to Maui in 1826. The larvae of *Culex quinquefasciatus* were

'Ua'u or Hawaiian Petrel
(Pterodroma sandwichensis).

Newell's Shearwater *(Puffinus newelli).*

residing in the freshwater casks of a ship named the *Wellington* that arrived in Lahaina after visiting San Blas, Mexico. Sailors dumped the water barrels into the streams, and several months later local Hawaiians began complaining about the insects that sung in their ears at night and were biting them. The mosquito's population increased rapidly and eventually some of them bit introduced birds, including caged birds, game birds, and chickens that were hosts of the parasite *Plasmodium relictum*, which affects red blood cells and causes avian malaria. The mosquitoes then bit the native Hawaiian birds. Most Hawaiian birds infected with malaria become weak, emaciated, and moribund. The disease frequently leads to death.

The first bird species introduced to Hawai'i was the Polynesian Jungle Fowl. Wild Turkeys *(Meleagris gallopavo)* along with several pair of pigeons, most likely Rock Doves *(Columba livia)*, were brought to the island of Hawai'i from China in 1788; these were the first bird species to be introduced to post-contact Hawai'i. By 1825 they were reported to be abundant in Honolulu.

From 1778 to 1962, a minimum of 142 bird species were intentionally released or escaped from captivity on O'ahu. Of these, ninety-four were unable to establish long-term viable populations on the island. Today forty-two alien land bird species are reproducing on O'ahu. This contrasts sadly with only five remaining native

Wild Turkeys *(Meleagris gallopavo)*.

Rock Dove *(Columba livia)*.

land bird species. Six exotic species, Varied Tit (*Parus varius*), California Quail (*Callipepla californica*), Chukar (*Alectoris Chukar*), Red Jungle Fowl, Wild Turkey (*Meleagris gallopavo*), and Gray-sided Laughingthrush (*Garrulax caerulatus*), established populations on Oʻahu but eventually became extinct.[26] Between the Hawaiʻi Board of Agriculture and Forestry, Hui Manu, and misguided citizens, Oʻahu became a menagerie of birds from all over the world. Absurdly out-of-place species were carelessly released on Oʻahu. Many of them carried alien diseases and parasites that would infect and harm the native birds.

California Quail *(Callipepla californica).*

Eventually some of the introduced species—including the Japanese White-eye (*Zosterops japonicas*), White-rumped Shama (*Copsychus malabaricus*), Red-billed Leiothrix (*Leiothrix lutea*), Red-whiskered Bulbul (*Pycnonotus jocosus*), Japanese Bush-Warbler (*Cettia diphone*), Northern Cardinal (*Cardinalis cardinalis*), and others—found their way into the forest areas, where they encountered the surviving honeycreepers. Today they are

Chukar *(Alectoris Chukar).*

Japanese White-eye
(*Zosterops japonicas*).

White-rumped Shama
(*Copsychus malabaricus*).

Red-billed Leiothrix (*Leiothrix lutea*).

Red-whiskered Bulbul
(*Pycnonotus jocosus*).

competing for the same insects and nectar that the native birds need to survive. Recent studies indicate the native Hawaiian forest birds are being adversely effected by the recent newcomers in their midst.

The regrettable results of the introduction of predators, grazing animals, mosquitoes, foreign birds, competition, disease, and degradation of habitat on Oʻahu have been massive extinctions and continuing severe reductions to the original flora and fauna that had evolved in isolation for 5 million years or longer.

Today Hawaiʻi is called both the "Extinction Capitol of the World" and the "Endangered Species Capitol of the World." The following chart clearly depicts the results of the devastation on Oʻahu's native land bird and flightless species.

Japanese Bush-Warbler *(Cettia diphone)*.

Northern Cardinal *(Cardinalis cardinalis)*.

Still present

Pueo
'Apapane
'Amakihi

Endangered

'I'iwi *(extremely endangered)*
'Elepaio

Extinct

(Historic)	Ziegler's Crake	Wahi Grosbeak
'Ō'ō	Ralph's Crake	King Kong Grosbeak
'Āmaui	Haliaeetus sp.	Oahu Koa Finch
Creeper	Buteo sp.	Ridge-Billed Finch
'Ākepa	Hawaiian Harrier	Hoopoe-billed
'Ō'ū	Oahu Stilt Owl	Akialoa
'Akialoa	Deep-Billed Crow	Straight-billed Gaper
Nuku pu'u	Slender-Billed Crow	Sickle-Billed Gaper
	Chaetoptila sp.	
(Subfossil)*	Laysan Finch *(extinct	** Extinct species are*
Oahu Moa-nalo	on O'ahu)*	*based on research*
Branta sp.	Makawehi Finch	*conducted by Storrs L.*
Supernumeray Oahu	Palila *(extinct on*	*Olson and Helen F. James*
Goose	O'ahu)*	

Of the thirty-four species that existed on the island before the arrival of humans around AD 1000, only five remain: the Hawaiian Short-eared Owl (pueo), the 'Amakihi, the 'Apapane, the 'I'iwi, and the 'Elepaio. The O'ahu population of 'I'iwi is extremely endangered, with fewer than ten birds surviving. The 'Elepaio has less than 1,200 birds remaining and is listed as endangered.[27] Only 6 percent of O'ahu's original land bird species remain, with viable but diminished populations. The severity of the loss of bird species is among the worst of any place in the history of our planet.

O'ahu's native plant species have also been decimated at an alarming rate. As of 2010, 122 plant species, 20 percent of the to-

'Amakihi

'Apapane

'I'iwi

'Elepaio

tal, were listed as endangered. All of the forty-one colorful native tree snail species of the genus *Achatinella* are currently classified as endangered, but only eleven species still actually exist. O'ahu's only native mammals—the Hawaiian bat and the Hawaiian monk seal—are listed as endangered species.

Efforts to Save the Few that Remain

During the last forty years, significant efforts have been made to understand and reduce the terrible loss of native species on O'ahu. The U.S. Fish and Wildlife Service has established several important national wildlife refuges on the island, and the State of Hawai'i Department of Forestry and Wildlife has created important natural area and forest reserves. The Ko'olau and Wai'anae Mountains Watershed Partnerships have been created to protect, restore, and enhance the native flora and fauna of these areas. The Invasive Species Committee is trying to prevent the establishment of new alien pests and to eradicate current pests. Many environmental nonprofit organizations have worked to improve and protect O'ahu's remaining natural habitats.

A fence has been built at Ka'ena Point to eliminate predators from this important and growing seabird colony.

Surveys and studies have been done to understand where the remaining Oʻahu ʻElepaio live and what they need to survive. Poison bait stations designed to kill rats have been established around their nesting locations in an effort to improve their reproduction. A fence has been built at Kaʻena Point to eliminate predators from this important and growing seabird colony. Additional fences have been and are being built in the Waiʻanae and Koʻolau ranges that will help keep grazing animals, feral pigs, and rats from eating endangered plants. Studies are ongoing that seek to find ways to stop the spread of avian malaria and other bird diseases. Endangered Hawaiian plant species are being raised in greenhouses and being planted into fenced enclosures. Native tree snails are being raised in a lab at the University of Hawaiʻi and reintroduced to the mountains. Nature itself is apparently adapting to the new threats. The Oʻahu ʻAmakihi and ʻElepaio have developed some resistance to avian malaria.

Future threats to the declining native species include the possible accidental introduction of the brown tree snake (*Boiga irregularis*) and other snakes and reptiles, more intentional releases of new bird species, the spread of invasive plant species farther into the remaining native forest areas, introduction of new insect species such as fire ants, and the arrival of other avian diseases, including the West Nile virus. Any of these could result in the eventual extinction of Oʻahu's last few remaining forest bird species.

Brown tree snake *(Boiga irregularis).*

Unfortunately, by the time Oʻahu's serious environmental problems were fully understood, most of the island's bird species were extinct. The native forests and plants had been reduced from covering 100 percent of the island to a few small areas in the higher mountains and along the coast. Today we are left with only very few survivors of what once represented some of the best examples of evolution on Earth. We need more public awareness and education, increased funding, and major efforts to save these last few species that cannot plead for their own salvation. If we permit the continued loss and eventual extinctions of what is left of the ancient and beautiful flora and fauna through widespread indifference and lack of support, future generations will inherit an island that has nothing but weeds, alien trees, foreign birds, rats, pigs, and museum collections (photographs and descriptions of the original and spectacular native species). What a tremendous waste and loss this would be.

Please do what you can to help Hawai'i's endangered species and habitats. Consider joining and volunteering for any of the nonprofit environmental groups listed in that section. Ask elected officials to seek more funding to protect the island's natural areas and endangered species. The remaining few are very important and deserve all of our best efforts to help them survive.

Places to Experience and Enjoy Nature on Oʻahu

Keaīwa Heiau State Recreation Area and ʻAiea Loop Trail

DISTANCE: 5 miles round-trip

TIME: Minimum 3 to 4 hours

HIGHLIGHTS: Oʻahu ʻAmakihi, Oʻahu ʻElepaio, ʻApapane, Marianas Swiftlet, sandalwood, remnant native forest, mountain scenery, and Hawaiian heiau.

DIRECTIONS: Follow the H-1 Freeway to Moanalua Highway (Hwy. 78). Take the ʻAiea cutoff to the third traffic light, make a right turn at ʻAiea Heights Drive, and follow it about 3 miles up to the end of the road. After you drive through the gate, continue forward and then stay right at the fork. Continue to the top of the road, where you will see the parking lot for the ʻAiea Trail.

NOTES: Bring plenty of water, leave no valuables in car, start early in the a.m., bring cellular phone and sunscreen. Be careful on the slippery, wet, and muddy trail that has exposed roots in some areas.

DONATION AND VOLUNTEER OPPORTUNITIES: Sierra Club Oʻahu, www.hi.sierraclub.org/OAHU/index.htm

Eucalyptus.

The 'Aiea Loop Trail is located in a forested area high above Pearl Harbor. From several lookout points you can see the southern coastline of O'ahu and the Wai'anae Range. This area was replanted by foresters in the late 1920s after uncontrolled grazing by cattle and goats destroyed almost all of the native vegetation. Eucalyptus, strawberry guava, and stands of Norfolk Island pine trees are common along the entire trail. You can walk the 4.8-mile loop or turn around at the halfway point, where a short spur trail leads to an overlook of the H-3 Freeway and Halawa Valley. Experienced hikers can walk up the 'Aiea Ridge

Acacia koa.

trail, which has the best remaining native forest in the area and offers great opportunities to see native birds.

As you walk up the path, you occasionally will see the surviving endemic *Acacia koa* trees. This species is the second most common tree in the native forest. Koa translates as "brave, bold, fearless warrior." They have sickle-shaped phyllodes, which are not leaves but flattened stems. The true leaves are very small and the flowers are pale yellow. Hawaiians used koa to make surfboards and outrigger canoes. Today the valuable wood is used to make bowls, boxes, cabinets, and countertops. Hawai'i's only endemic butterfly species, the Kamehameha butterfly (*Vanessa tameamea*), and Blackburn's little blue butterfly (*Udara blackburni*) both use the sap of the koa for food, and the endemic koa bugs eat the seeds.

Kamehameha butterfly *(Vanessa tameamea)*.

Blackburn's little blue butterfly *(Udara blackburni)*.

The most common native tree is the 'ōhi'a lehua (*Metrosideros polymorpha*). Look for the bright red flowers. The 'Apapane (*Himati-*

'Ōhi'a lehua *(Metrosideros polymorpha)*.

'Apapane *(Himatione sanguine sanguineai)*.

one sanguine sanguineai) and O'ahu 'Amakihi *(Chlorodrepanis flavus)* will visit the flowers when they are producing nectar. If you find the honeycreepers in a particular tree, you can wait for them to return again to get more nectar every twenty to thirty minutes. Be careful that you don't confuse the abundant alien Japanese White-eye *(Zosterops japonicas)* for the similar looking 'Amakihi. Hawaiians used 'ōhi'a wood to make idols, weapons, tool handles, and boards for making poi. These trees have very tiny seeds that are wind dispersed.

Look for the small red berries of the pūki-awe *(Styphelia tameiam-eiae)* along the midsection of the trail. This species is indigenous to Hawai'i and the Marquesas Islands. A few remnant 'iliahi or sandalwood *(Santalum frey-cinetianum)* trees also occur on the 'Aiea Loop Trail. Notice the drooping leaves and very small, reddish-yellow

O'ahu 'Amakihi *(Chlorodrepanis flavus)*.

Japanese White-eye *(Zosterops japonicas)*.

flowers. Hawaiians used various parts of the trees for medicine, perfume, firewood, and musical instruments. Great quantities of sandalwood trees were cut down on Oʻahu and the other Hawaiian Islands and sent to China from 1791 to 1839. In Asia, the dried heartwood was used to make idols and sacred utensils for shrines, carvings, boxes, and incense. By 1840 most of the easily accessible sandalwood had been removed and the industry collapsed.

Pūkiawe *(Styphelia tameiameiae).*

Several hundred years ago, many extinct species of endemic Hawaiian birds—including the ʻŌʻū *(Psittirostra psittacea)*, Greater ʻAkialoa *(Akialoa ellisiana ellisiana)*, Nuku puʻu *(Hemignathus lucidus lucidus)*, ʻAkepa *(Loxops coccineus wolstenholmei)*, Oʻahu ʻŌʻō *(moho apicalis)*, and others—would have been present in the trees along this trail, but today only old field notes and fading museum skins remain as witness to their former existence.

ʻIliahi or sandalwood *(Santalum freycinetianum).*

Two other bird species have been observed on Oʻahu in recent years and could be found on the ʻAiea Loop Trail and surrounding areas with exceptional luck. One is extremely rare and the other most likely extinct. ʻIʻiwi *(Vestiaria coccinea)* were sighted in the

Wai'anae Range in 2008, 2009, and 2013, and a small population of six birds was documented in the northern Ko'olau Range in 1996. The last well-documented sighting of the O'ahu 'Alauahio or O'ahu Creeper *(Paroreomyza maculata)* was of two birds in 1985 not far from the 'Aiea Loop Trail. [28]

As noted earlier, most of O'ahu's endemic forest birds have been devastated. The few species that have survived this avian catastrophe cling to a precarious existence in forests that are declining. One of the best places to look for the O'ahu 'Amakihi, 'Apapane, and the endangered O'ahu 'Elepaio *(Chasiempis ibidis)* is on the 'Aiea Loop Trail. The 'Amakihi and 'Apapane are survivors partly because they have adapted to feeding on introduced species,

Extinct O'ahu forest birds: (top to bottom) 'Akepa *(Loxops coccineus wolstenholmei)*, 'Amaui *(Myadestes woahensis)*, Nuku pu'u *(Hemignathus lucidus lucidus)*, 'O'ū *(Psittirostra psittacea)*, Greater 'Akialoa *(Akialoa ellisiana ellisiana)*, and 'Ō'ō *(moho apicalis)*.

'I'iwi *(Vestiaria coccinea)*

O'ahu 'Elepaio *(Chasiempis ibidis)*.

O'ahu 'Alauahio or O'ahu Creeper
(Paroreomyza maculata).

including Lantana camara, Schefflera actinophylla, many eucalyptus species, and others. The islandwide populations of the only remaining honeycreepers on O'ahu are unknown due to a lack of recent surveys. The O'ahu 'Elepaio is an endangered species and fewer than 1,200 birds remain. Their numbers have plummeted because of avian diseases, predation, loss of habitat, and competition with introduced birds.

One other bird to watch for on the 'Aiea Loop Trail is the rare Mariana Swiftlet *(Aerodramus bartschi)*. In May 1962, 125 to 175 birds were released from Guam into a valley in southeast O'ahu. Seven years later a population was documented in North Halawa Valley. In 1978, their nesting site was discovered in the same valley. [29] In 2000, forty-nine active nests were counted. The swiftlets are very fast, and most of the observations last only a few seconds as the bird races by. Look for this endangered species where you have good vantage

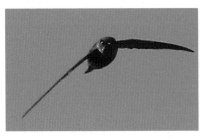

Mariana Swiftlet *(Aerodramus bartschi)*.

places along the trail with a lot of open sky. Several other rare introduced birds have been seen on the ʻAiea Loop Trail. The melodious Chinese Laughingthrush or Hwamei *(Garrulax canorus)* is native to China and was introduced to Hawaiʻi sometime before 1900. They are very secretive and are rarely seen. The Yellow-faced Grassquit *(Tiaris olivaceus)* has occurred in this area in the past but is extremely rare today.

Chinese Laughingthrush or Hwamei *(Garrulax canorus).*

The Keaīwa Heiau was used by kāhuna lapaʻau, highly regarded ancient practitioners, who used plants to cure illnesses. Many of the species used in traditional herbal medicines still grow in the area. It was built in the sixteenth century by Kakuhihewa, an aliʻi or chief of Oʻahu. The rock-walled heiau or temple is 4 feet high, 100 feet wide, and 160 feet long.

Yellow-faced Grassquit *(Tiaris olivaceus).*

Mānoa Cliff Trail

DISTANCE: 4.6 miles round-trip

TIME: Minimum 3 to 4 hours

HIGHLIGHTS: Oʻahu ʻAmakihi, ʻApapane, lobelias, remnant native forest, restoration area, and mountain scenery.

DIRECTIONS: Proceed up Round Top Drive, past Puʻu ʻUalakaʻa State Park. Continue driving up the road until you see brown and yellow trailhead signs along the side of the road. Mānoa Cliff Trail's parking lot is on the left side of Round Top Drive. The trail begins across the street from the lot.

NOTES: Bring water, leave no valuables in car, bring cellular phone and sunscreen. Be careful on the slippery, wet, and muddy trail that has exposed roots in some areas.

DONATION AND VOLUNTEER OPPORTUNITIES: The Mānoa Cliff Forest Restoration Project, manoacliffreforestation.wordpress.com or info@manoacliff.org

The trail begins in an introduced swamp mahogany forest. Near the top of the steps, you reach a strawberry guava section that is often muddy. After another 50 yards, the trail descends, offering a spectacular view of Mānoa Valley. Be careful in this section due to slippery conditions. The trail contours the cliffs above Mānoa Valley and around Tantalus Crater to Pauoa Valley. Look for several waterfalls in the back of the valley on rainy days. This is the best trail close to Honolulu to see a great variety of native Hawaiian forest plant species, including several island of Oʻahu endemic species.

Hala pepe *(Pleomele halapepe).*

Watch for hala pepe *(Pleomele halapepe)* on the right of the trail. This species is found only

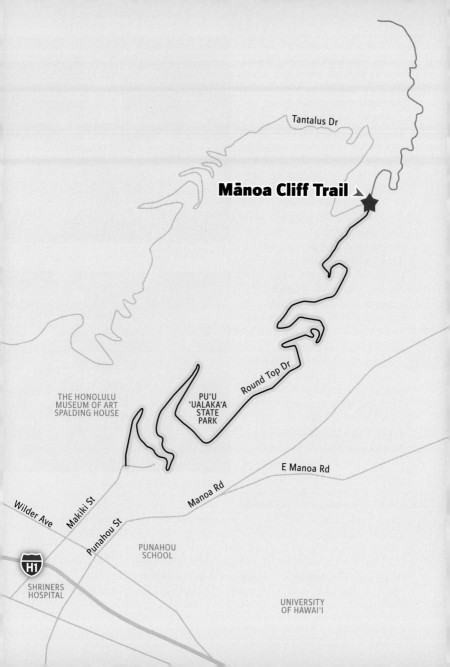

on Oʻahu and nowhere else on Earth. Practitioners of Hawaiian traditional medicine used the bark and leaves of this tree, blended with other plant ingredients, to cure fever, chills, and lung disorders. Hala pepe represents the hula goddess Kapo and is placed in buildings where hula is taught or performed.

The colorful flowers and fruit of the climbing vine ʻieʻie (*Freycinetia arborea*) can be seen in several places along the trail. This fruit was a primary food of the now extinct ʻŌʻū (*Psittirostra psittacea*). Native Hawaiians use parts of the ʻieʻie to make fish traps, baskets, and the framework for feather-covered helmets and cloaks.

ʻIeʻie *(Freycinetia arborea)*.

Look for the tiny white flowers of the Hawaiian endemic kōpiko (*Psychotria mariniana*). This species is a member of the coffee family. The hard wood of kōpiko was used by Hawaiians to make anvils and for fuel.

Perhaps the most beautiful native tree on this trail is the Oʻahu endemic kokiʻo keʻokeʻo (*Hibiscus arnottianus*). These trees

Kōpiko *(Psychotria mariniana)*.

grow from 15 to 30 feet tall and have spectacular white flowers with pink or red staminal columns. They bloom year-round and are the only known species of hibiscus in the world that has fragrant flowers.

Look for the small red flowers of ʻāhihi (*Metrosideros tremuloides*), another Oʻahu endemic tree species that grows along this trail. The specific epithet tremuloides means "to tremble," in reference to the

Kokiʻo keʻokeʻo *(Hibiscus arnottianus)*.

ʻĀhihi *(Metrosideros tremuloides)*.

Mamaki *(Pipturus albidus)*.

Olonā *(Touchardia latifolia)*.

leaves trembling in the wind. The flowers were used to make leis.

Unfortunately, many introduced weedy species are also found on this trail and compete with the native plants for sunlight, space, and nutrients. Some good examples of the koa and 'ōhi'a lehua trees occur on the hillsides above and below the path. The Mānoa Cliff Trail is a good place to view both the O'ahu 'Amakihi and 'Apapane. If you see any of the exotic octopus or umbrella trees *(Schefflera actinophylla)* flowering, wait and watch for the birds to visit.

One of the most important forest plants for Native Hawaiians was the mamaki *(Pipturus albidus)*. The leaves were used to make a medicinal tea. Fibers were used to make bark cloth and rope. This interesting species is a member of the nettle family and lost its stinging qualities due to the lack of grazing animals in Hawai'i before 1778. Olonā *(Touchardia latifolia)*, another member of the nettle family, was an important plant used in early Hawaiian culture. Very strong fibers called laticifers were used by Hawaiians to make rope and nets.

As you walk farther on the trail, eventually you will find a bench. This is a excellent place to rest and enjoy the tremendous views of the upper Mānoa Valley. Far below is Lyon Arboretum, operated by the University of Hawai'i.

Continuing farther, you will reach the entry gate of the Mānoa Cliff Restoration Area. This is a great place to see how a small area of native forest is being restored through the efforts of dedicated volunteers and the State of Hawai'i. The project began in 2005, and a fence to keep out feral pigs was constructed around 6 acres of the site in 2009.

In this sanctuary you can see several species of lobelias, including *Clermontia kakeana* and *Cyanea angustifolia*. These plants are the most accessible in the Honolulu area. *Clermontia* are branched shrubs or small trees, up to 20 feet tall, with fleshy fruits. *Cyanea* is the largest and most diverse group of Hawaiian lobelioids, with more than 70 species. Many species are

Mānoa Cliff Restoration Area entry gate.

Clermontia kakeana.

Cyanea angustifolia.

now extinct. The common ancestor of all Hawaiian lobelia species arrived in the Hawaiian Islands about 13 million years ago.

Look for the small yellow flowers of the Oʻahu endemic koʻokoʻolau *(Bidens asymetrica)* in this location. This species is a member of the aster or sunflower family. The leaves were used to make a medicinal tea.

Gaze over the weedy ginger, just before the Puʻu ʻŌʻhia junction, for a view of Kāneʻohe in the distance. This trail intersects two other trails. The first intersection is the Puʻu ʻŌʻhia Trail on the left. The second intersection is the Pauoa Flats Trail on the right. It is best to turn around and walk back the same way rather than continuing, unless you know the trail system well. Unfortunately, many hikers have become lost in this area.

Koʻokoʻolau *(Bidens asymetrica).*

Segment of the Koʻolau volcano from 10 miles offshore.

Offshore Honolulu Pelagic Trip

DISTANCE: 40 to 50 Miles

TIME: 6 to 8 hours

HIGHLIGHTS: Spectacular coastal scenery from offshore perspective. Migratory and resident seabirds. Marine mammals including whales, dolphins, and sharks occasionally.

DIRECTIONS: Pelagic birding and nature tours can be reserved through www.hawaiibirdingtours.com.

NOTES: Wear sunscreen and hat. Have medicine for seasickness if needed.

DONATION AND VOLUNTEER OPPORTUNITIES: American Bird Conservancy: www.abcbirds.org/ (1-888-247-3624) Surfrider Foundation: oahu.surfrider.org/ (1-808-942-3841)

In order to escape the frustrations caused by all of the closed and restricted access refuges, preserves, and other areas on Oʻahu, there is nothing better than an exhilarating six-to-eight-hour boat trip 25 miles offshore of Oʻahu. Missing are the fences, the no trespassing or closed signs, the barbed wire—just the wild, open, and inviting

Mottled Petrel
(Pterodroma inexpectata).

ocean. Sailing at dawn toward the distant, glowing horizon searching for rare seabirds and marine mammals is a great experience you should definitely try. On many days, after reaching the 20-mile mark, O'ahu is barely visible. The far-off Wai'anae and Ko'olau volcanoes' shield shape becomes more apparent from this long-distance vantage point. Using your imagination, you can visualize what Captain Cook observed just after daybreak on January 18, 1778, when he discovered O'ahu for the outside world.

Many species of migrating seabirds fly every year from their breeding colonies in the southern hemisphere across the equator all the way to the waters off the western United States, Alaska, and Siberia. These epic journeys usually begin in March, with April being the high point. After spending late spring and summer in their northern feeding grounds, the birds fly rapidly thousands of miles back home in the fall. Details about the precise timing of their movements and their migration routes are still being learned. Every time you venture offshore searching for these rare

Black-winged Petrel
(Pterodroma nigripennis).

Stejneger Petrel *(Pterodroma longirostris).*

and unusual species is an opportunity to discover something new and to contribute as citizen scientists toward a better understanding of these birds' uncharted pathways. For the most part, they are deep-ocean wanderers and only rarely fly close to the coastline of O'ahu.

One of the most impressive groups of birds to be found on a pelagic trip off Honolulu are the graceful and agile petrels. Species that occasionally are observed include the midsize, transequatorial migrating Mottled Petrel (*Pterodroma inexpectata*), the Black-winged Petrel (*Pterodroma nigripennis*), Cook Petrel (*Pterodroma cookii*), and the Stejneger Petrel (*Pterodroma longirostris*). They feed on food items picked from the surface, but when flying by the Hawaiian Islands they are usually going very fast without stopping.

The larger Hawaiian Petrel (*Pterodroma sandwichensis*) is resident and nests on Kaua'i, Moloka'i, Maui, Lāna'i, and Hawai'i. This endangered species has been recorded off O'ahu occasionally. Another state breeding bird is the small Bulwer Petrel (*Bulweria bulwerii*), which nests on O'ahu but is rarely seen close to shore. The very rare Kermadec Petrel (*Pterodroma neglecta*) has been seen only seven times in

Hawaiian Petrel
(Pterodroma sandwichensis).

Bulwer Petrel *(Bulweria bulwerii).*

Kermadec Petrel *(Pterodroma neglecta).*

Leach Storm-Petrel
(*Oceanodroma leucorhoa*).

Band-rumped Storm-Petrel
(*Oceanodroma castro*).

Sooty Shearwater (*Puffinus griseus*).

Pomarine Jaeger
(*Stercorarius pomarinus*).

the southeastern Hawaiian Islands.

Several species of diminutive Storm-Petrels, including Leach Petrel *(Oceanodroma leucorhoa)* and Band-rumped *(Oceanodroma castro)*, can be encountered during a day trip off O'ahu, but sightings are rare. On April 21, 2013, an astonishing thirty-five Storm-Petrels were recorded between 10 and 25 miles offshore of Waikīkī during an unusually calm day when the Kona winds were less than 5 knots and the ocean surface was smooth as glass.

Red Phalarope *(Phalaropus fulicarius)*.

Sooty Shearwater *(Puffinus griseus)*, Pomarine Jaeger *(Stercorarius pomarinus)*, Red Phalarope *(Phalaropus fulicarius)*, Red-tailed Tropic-

Red-tailed Tropicbird *(Phaethon rubricaudai)*.

Red-billed Tropicbird *(Phaethon aethereus)*.

Short-finned pilot whale
(*Globicephala macrorhynchus*).

Spinner dolphins (*Stenella longirostris*).

bird *(Phaethon rubricaudai)*, and very rare Red-billed Tropicbird *(Phaethon aethereus)*, in addition to many resident seabird species, can all be seen on these exciting trips. Every so often, flying fish will break the surface, or a group of short-finned pilot whales *(Globicephala macrorhynchus)* will be sighted. One of the most thrilling experiences is encountering a pod of performing spinner dolphins *(Stenella longirostris)* that seem to thoroughly enjoy riding the bow wave and showing off their incredible swimming abilities. Altogether, forty different species of seabirds have been observed in the waters surrounding Oʻahu, so these are great places to go if you want to enjoy nature at its best while visiting or living on the island.

Kapi'olani Park

DISTANCE: 1/4-mile

TIME: 1 hour

HIGHLIGHTS: White Tern *(Gygis alba)*, Pacific Golden-Plover *(Pluvialis fulva)*, and many introduced bird species.

DIRECTIONS: Located in Honolulu, at the east end of Waikīkī, just beyond Kuhio Beach Park.

NOTES: Wear sunscreen and hat.

DONATION AND VOLUNTEER OPPORTUNITIES: None at present.

Kapi'olani Park is the largest and oldest public park in the state. The 300-acre park was named after Queen Kapi'olani, the wife of Hawai'i's last king, David Kalākaua. It opened on June 11, 1877. The park is a great place to watch the graceful and elegant White Tern. Be sure to check the branches of the giant Indian banyan trees

White Tern.

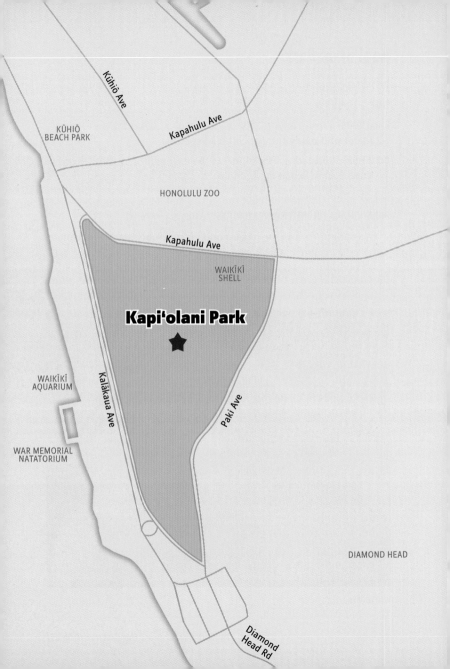

Pacific Golden-Plover.

for both adults and young chicks. The entire population of over six hundred birds lives in southeast Oʻahu, and they are rarely observed on the other islands in Hawaiʻi.

Look for the beautiful Pacific Golden-Plover in the grassy areas. This incredible bird migrates every year back and forth between Hawaiʻi and its breeding grounds in the Arctic. They are present from late July until late April and spend about nine months of their life every year in Hawaiʻi.

This location is a great place to see what I call the "United Nations" of Hawaiian birds. Introduced species from four continents reside here. One of the most conspicuous is the large, Cattle Egret *(Bubulcus ibis)*, which was brought to Hawaiʻi from Florida in 1959 to help control insects that were affecting cattle. Two varieties of

Cattle Egret *(Bubulcus ibis).*

Spotted Dove
(Streptopelia chinensis).

Zebra or Barred Dove
(Geopelia striata).

dove from Asia, the Spotted Dove *(Streptopelia chinensis)* and Zebra or Barred Dove *(Geopelia striata)*, can easily be seen. Several parakeet species have been observed in and around the park area. The Rose-ringed Parakeet *(Psittacula krameri)* naturally occurs in Africa and Asia. They were first noticed on Oʻahu in the 1930s and the flock today has increased to over seven hundred birds. Red-masked Parakeets *(Aratinga erythrogenys)*, native to South America, roost at the

Rose-ringed Parakeet *(Psittacula krameri).*

Red-masked Parakeet
(Aratinga erythrogenys).

Doris Duke Estate and occasionally fly over the park as they search for food.

The Red-vented Bulbuls *(Pycnonotus cafer)* are very common at Kapi'olani Park. This species is considered an agricultural pest and were first observed on O'ahu in 1966. Several other birds introduced from Asia are seen in the park often. These include the Scaly-breasted Munia *(Lonchura punctulata)*, Java Sparrow *(Padda oryzivora)*, Chestnut Munia *(Lonchura atricapilla)*, and Common Myna *(Acridotheres tristis)*. The House Finch *(Carpodacus mexicanus)* and English Sparrow *(Passer domesticus)* both thrive here. This is one of the best places on O'ahu to see the Yellow-fronted Canary *(Serinus mozambicus)* from Africa.

Several species of birds that are found on O'ahu could someday

Red-vented Bulbul
(Pycnonotus cafer).

Scaly-breasted Munia
(Lonchura punctulata).

Java Sparrow *(Padda oryzivora)*.

Chestnut Munia *(Lonchura atricapilla)*.

Common Myna (*Acridotheres tristis*).

House Finch
(*Carpodacus mexicanus*).

English Sparrow (*Passer domesticus*).

Yellow-fronted Canary
(*Serinus mozambicus*).

The Red-whiskered Bulbul
(*Pycnonotus jocosus*).

Saffron Finch (*Sicalis flaveola*).

expand their range to include Kapi'olani Park. The Red-whiskered Bulbul *(Pycnonotus jocosus)* occurs mostly in the mountains, but some of these pest birds live in the lowland areas on O'ahu. The beautiful Saffron Finch *(Sicalis flaveola)* from South America is mainly found in areas around Pearl Harbor but with favorable conditions could expand its range to southeast O'ahu.

Red-crested Cardinal *(Paroaria coronate).*

Beginning in the late 1920s, a group of affluent citizens in Honolulu formed a bird society called Hui Manu (manu is the Hawaiian word for bird). They brought in species from around the world to repopulate the island with singing birds after the native birds had declined and to help control insects. Two of the most common species in the park; the Red-crested Cardinal *(Paroaria coronate)* from South America and the Common Waxbill *(Estrilda astrild)* from Africa are examples of successful introductions but other additions to O'ahu's alien birdlife were not so fortunate. Many species of exotic birds were recorded in the park area during the 1960s that had been released from cages onto the slopes of Diamond Head Crater. These included the Pin-tailed Whydah *(Vidua macroura)*, African Firefinch *(Lagonosticta rubricata)*, Red Bishop

Common Waxbill *(Estrilda astrild).*

Lavender Waxbill *(Estrilda caerulescens).*

Orange-cheeked Waxbill *(Estrilda melpoda)*.

(Euplectis orix), White-rumped Seedeater *(Serinus leucopygius)*, Baya Weaver *(Ploceus philippinus)*, Blue-capped Cordonbleu *(Uraeginthus cyanocephalus)*, and Red-cheeked Cordonbleu *(Uraeginthus bengalus)*. Most of these species lasted only ten or twenty years before they disappeared from the area. Two other species that were included in these introductions, the Lavender Waxbill *(Estrilda caerulescens)* the and Orange-cheeked Waxbill *(Estrilda melpoda)*, persisted in the Kapi'olani Park area until the late 1980s. Today the Lavender Waxbill can sometimes be found in Wailupe Valley in southeast O'ahu, and the Orange-cheeked Waxbill still exists, with a very small population in Kāne'ohe.

If you visit the park at night, you might see the few resident Barn Owls *(Tyto alba)* that live in the area. The owls were introduced to Hawai'i in 1958 in an effort to control rats and mice that were causing damage on agricultural land.

Barn Owl *(Tyto alba)*.

Hanauma Bay

TIME: 2 to 3 hours

HIGHLIGHTS: Marine life, excellent coastal scenery.

DIRECTIONS: Driving from Honolulu, proceed east on Kalaniana'ole Highway past Hawai'i Kai. Continue driving until you see a driveway on your right. This is the entrance to the parking lot.

NOTES: Arrive early to avoid crowds. Leave no valuables in car. Please do not feed the fish. Wear sunscreen and hat. Be aware of ocean conditions. Closed on Tuesday.

DONATION AND VOLUNTEER OPPORTUNITIES: Friends of Hanauma Bay: www.friendsofhanaumabay.org/

About 30,000 years ago, volcanic activity occurred along the southeast flank of the Ko'olau Volcano. Water came into contact with

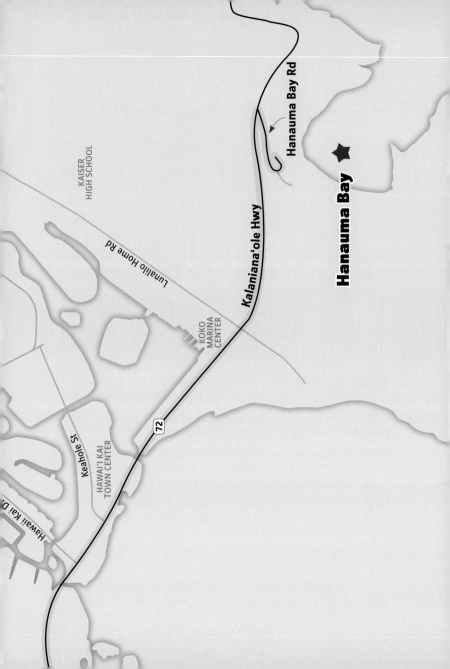

KAISER
HIGH SCHOOL

Hanauma Bay Rd

Hanauma Bay

Kalaniana'ole Hwy

Lunalilo Home Rd

KOKO
MARINA
CENTER

72

Keahole St.

HAWAI'I KAI
TOWN CENTER

Hawaii Kai Dr.

underground magma and created steam explosions. Material was ejected high into the air, then fell back to create several circular-shaped tuff cones. Eventually part of the crater's wall collapsed, allowing ocean water to enter. Over time, a coral reef developed inside the cone. [30]

Hanauma translates as "curved bay" or "arm-wrestling bay." It was a favorite fishing location of King Kamehameha V and in 1967 was designated a Marine Life Conservation District. Today it is one of the best places to observe Hawai'i's beautiful marine life.

Opportunities are very good at Hanauma Bay for both novice and experienced snorkelers and scuba divers. Close to shore, in water only 4 to 9 feet deep, you can see lobe coral *(Porites lobata)*, which is the most common species of coral in Hawai'i. Additional coral species growing here include cauliflower coral *(Pocillopora me-*

Lobe coral *(Porites lobata).*

Cauliflower coral *(Pocillopora meandrina).*

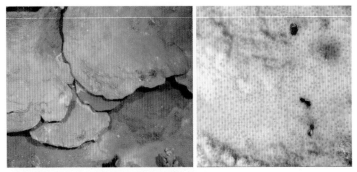

Spreading or sandpaper coral *(Montipora patula)*.

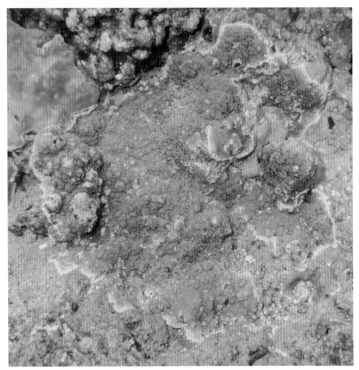

Blue rice coral *(Montipora flabellata)*.

andrina), spreading or sandpaper coral *(Montipora patula),* and blue rice coral *(Montipora flabellata).* In deeper water, finger coral *(Porites compressa),* the second most common coral species in Hawai'i, can be seen.

Common fish species in the shallow water areas include Hawaiian Sergeant *(Abudefduf abdominalis),* Brown Surgeonfish *(Acanthurus nigrofuscus),* Milletseed Butterflyfish *(Chaetodon miliaris),* Goldring Surgeonfish *(Ctenochaetus strigosus),* Belted Wrasse *(Stethojulis balteata),* and Saddle Wrasse *(Thalassoma duperrey).*

Hawaiian Sergeant
(Abudefduf abdominalis).

Brown Surgeonfish
(Acanthurus nigrofuscus).

Milletseed Butterflyfish
(Chaetodon miliaris).

Goldring Surgeonfish
(Ctenochaetus strigosus).

Belted Wrasse *(Stethojulis balteata).*   Saddle Wrasse *(Thalassoma duperrey).*

Hawaiian Whitespotted Toby
(Canthigaster jactator).   Oval Chromis *(Chromis ovalis).*

If you swim farther from shore into deeper water, other fish species can be observed. These include the Hawaiian Whitespotted Toby *(Canthigaster jactator)*, Oval Chromis *(Chromis ovalis)*, Vanderbilt Chromis *(Chromis vanderbilti)*, Hawaiian Dascyllus *(Dascyllus albisella)*, Bluestripe Snapper *(Lutjanus kasmira)*, Sleek Unicornfish *(Naso hexacanthus)*, and Johnston Island Damselfish *(Plectroglyphidodon Johnstonianus)*.

One of the highlights of visiting Hanauma Bay is sighting green sea turtles, or honu *(Chelonia mydas)*, resting or feeding in the near-shore water. The turtles are a threatened species and were hunted as recently as 1975.

Vanderbilt Chromis *(Chromis vanderbilti)*.

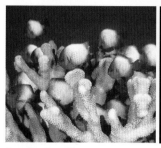

Hawaiian Dascyllus
(Dascyllus albisella).

Bluestripe Snapper *(Lutjanus kasmira)*.

Sleek Unicornfish *(Naso hexacanthus)*.

Johnston Island Damselfish
*(Plectroglyphidodon
Johnstonianus)*.

Ka'iwi Scenic Shoreline

DISTANCE: 1 mile

TIME: 2 hours

HIGHLIGHTS: Native plants, excellent coastal scenery.

DIRECTIONS: Driving from Honolulu, proceed east on Kalaniana'ole Highway past Sandy Beach. Continue driving until you see a driveway on your right with a gate. This is the entrance to the parking lot. If you arrive before 7 a.m., you can park along the highway. If driving from Kāne'ohe or Kailua, proceed on Kalaniana'ole Highway past Waimānalo and Sea Life Park. Continue past the top of the hill and the Makapu'u Lookout until you see the driveway on your left.

NOTES: Leave no valuables in car. Start early in the a.m. Please do not walk on native plants. Wear sunscreen and hat.

DONATION AND VOLUNTEER OPPORTUNITIES: Livable Hawai'i Kai Hui: www.old.hawaiikaihui.org/4436.html

Lava flows from Kalama Crater covered much of this area about 30,000 years ago. Subsequent wave action reshaped this shoreline and deposited sand and cobble beaches. Native Hawaiians lived in this area for centuries, and a significant number of house sites, rock walls, fishing shrines, and sections of a 15 to 16-foot-wide stone-paved road known as the "Kings Highway" were documented by early 1930s archaeological studies. The old stone road was built during the reign of Kamehameha III, sometime after 1825. In 1984, archaeologists conducted another survey of the area but found only remnants of the old road. It is believed that the massive 35-foot-high tsunami waves that struck this coastal area in 1946 destroyed the other surface sites.

In 1932, Alan Davis leased most of the land in this area, built his home, and started Wāwāmalu cattle ranch. The relaxed living and serenity Alan and his family enjoyed at his coastal estate lasted fourteen years, until the tsunami on April Fool's Day of 1946 demolished everything. Developers were interested in building at Ka'iwi from the 1950s through the 1990s, but this beautiful coastline has been preserved thanks to groups of concerned citizens who fought for many years against these projects.

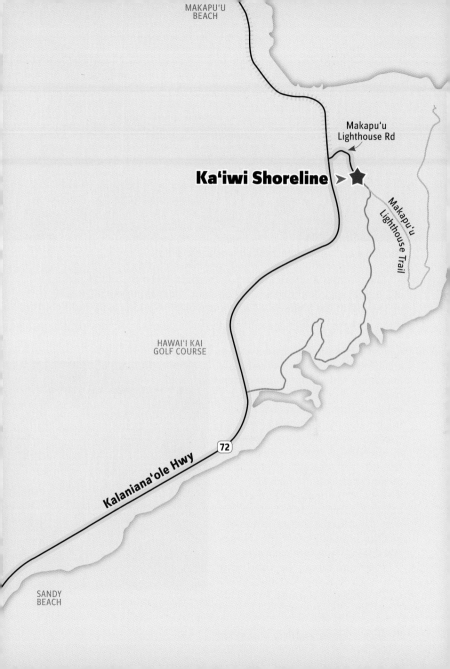

"Kings Highway," an old stone road built sometime after 1825.

Look for the dirt trail located on the right at the end of the parking lot that leads to the coastal area below. The main road/trail leads up the hill to the Makapu'u Lighthouse. After walking a short distance, you will start seeing groups of small shrubs with light gray-green leaves and yellow flowers. These are the endemic ma'o *(Gossypium tomentosum)*. Considered rare on O'ahu today, they grow only in a few areas. This is the native cotton plant. The short brownish fibers on the seeds are not commercially useful, but this plant's genes have been used in cotton-breeding programs in attempts to improve disease resistance and drought tolerance in commercial cotton varieties. The flowers of the ma'o were used for making beautiful leis and yellow dye. This scenic coastal area has healthy populations of the indigenous naio *(Myoporum sandwicense)*.

Continue along the trail until you reach Kaho'ohahai Inlet. Pele's Chair or Kapaliokamoa ("the cliff

Ma'o *(Gossypium tomentosum)*.

of the chicken") is the large lava rock formation above this picturesque coastal area. Check the tide pools along this coast for indigenous shallow-water fish species including the Zebra Blenny (*Istilblennius zebra*) and Dusky Frillgoby (*Bathygobius fuscus*). Juveniles of many Hawaiian reef fish species also inhabit the tide pools.

You can walk along the coast to the other side of this area by turning right at the ocean. The trail meanders around Ka'ili'ili Bay and Kaloko Inlet and ends near the highway past Kaloko Point.

Naio *(Myoporum sandwicense)*.

One of the botanical highlights of the area is the rare endemic hinahina kahakai (*Nama sandwicensis*). Found here and only one other place on O'ahu, it has very small blue flowers and succulent leaves. Growing nearby are elegant stands of hinahina (*Heliotropium anamolum*) and alena (*Boerhavia repens*). You can identify the hinahina by its conspicuous tiny white flowers and the one-half to one inch green-gray leaves. The flowers were used in lei making, and a medicinal tea was made from parts of this plant. Very small, pinkish tubular flowers are found on

Hinahina kahakai *(Nama sandwicensis)*.

Hinahina *(Heliotropium anamolum).* Alena *(Boerhavia repens).*

the herb alena. The sticky seeds of this species were most likely carried to Hawai'i by birds.

African Silverbills *(Lonchura cantans)*, previously called the warbling silverbill, inhabit this area but are difficult to find. This species was introduced to Hawai'i in the mid-1960s, and the first birds were

'Iwa or Great Frigatebird *(Fregata minor).*

◄ African Silverbills *(Lonchura cantans).*

observed at Ka'iwi in 1984. The 'iwa or Great Frigatebird *(Fregata minor)*, one of Hawai'i's largest birds with a seven-foot wingspan, can occasionally be spotted soaring over the area, usually flying from west to east. These incredible birds have some of the lightest bones of any bird species on Earth. All of the 'iwa breed in the Northwestern Hawaiian Islands, with the single exception of one historical nest at Moku Manu islet off Kāne'ohe in the summer of 1970. Over a thousand birds of this species roost on the same islet.

Red-breasted Merganser *(Mergus serrator).*

The extremely rare Red-breasted Merganser *(Mergus serrator)* was observed feeding on small fish in the tide pools along this shoreline in 2011. In April 2012 an even rarer Surfbird *(Aphriza virgata)* was seen along the nearby coast. This was

Surfbird *(Aphriza virgata).*

the first time in postcontact Hawaiian history, a period of 234 years, that this species was found in the state.

Mānana and Kāohikaipu, two offshore islands.

Makapuʻu Beach Park

DISTANCE: 200 yards

TIME: 1 hour

HIGHLIGHTS: Offshore seabird sanctuaries, recent lava flow, Red-footed Boobies, native plants, excellent coastal scenery.

DIRECTIONS: Driving from Honolulu, proceed east on Kalanianaʻole Highway past Sandy Beach. Continue driving past the Makapuʻu lookout at the top of the hill, where there is a spectacular view of Windward Oʻahu. Continue to the bottom of the hill and then turn right into Makapuʻu Beach Park. The entrance is on the ocean side of the highway across from the Sea Life Park entrance. It is best to park in the lot and walk the area to the north along the coast, going in the opposite direction of the lighthouse and Makapuʻu Point. Excellent native plant areas can be found right next to the parking lot. If driving from Kāneʻohe or Kailua,

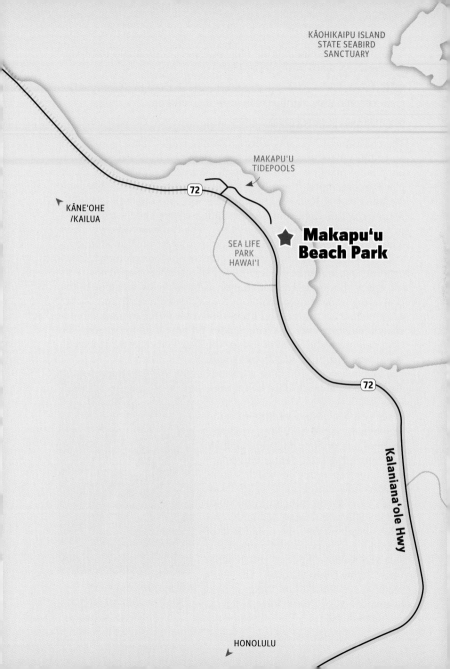

KĀOHIKAIPU ISLAND
STATE SEABIRD
SANCTUARY

MAKAPUʻU
TIDEPOOLS

72

KĀNEʻOHE
/KAILUA

SEA LIFE
PARK
HAWAIʻI

★ **Makapuʻu
Beach Park**

72

Kalanianaʻole Hwy

HONOLULU

proceed on Kalaniana'ole Highway past Waimānalo until you reach the beach park on your left.

NOTES: Leave no valuables in car. Start early in the a.m. Please do not walk on native plants. Wear sunscreen and hat.

DONATION AND VOLUNTEER OPPORTUNITIES: American Bird Conservancy.

The coastline at Makapu'u Beach Park is one of the few areas left on O'ahu where you can see a great assortment of native Hawaiian coastal plants and some incredible scenery. This is an excellent place to contemplate the different types of volcanic events that were included in the Honolulu Volcanic Series. Two offshore islands—Mānana, a tuff cone, and Kāohikaipu, a cinder cone—are seabird preserves and are closed to the public. The tuff cone was produced when water below the surface came in contact with molten lava. Steam was created and eventually great explosions occurred. Huge columns of ash rose high into the sky. The circular-shaped cone was formed with most of the material on the downwind side due to the prevailing trade winds. Kāohikaipu was created on dry land during a lower stand of the sea, and its reddish color is due to the combination of moisture and oxidizing gasses present at its formation. The land you are walking on is part of the Kaupō lava flow, which has been dated to only 30,000 years ago. The lava emerged from a vent 250 feet above sea level on the cliff behind Sea Life Park.[31]

If you are able visit this location at dawn in April and May, you will witness one of Hawai'i's most incredible bird displays. Bring binoculars or a spotting scope to watch a continuous movement of tens of thousands of birds as they fly from Moku Manu, Ulupa'u Crater, Mānana, and other locations past the ocean side of Mānana and around Makapu'u Point into the Ka'iwi Channel, which separates O'ahu from Moloka'i. The great majority of birds are Wedge-tailed Shearwaters or 'ua'u kani *(Puffinus*

Wedge-tailed Shearwater or 'ua'u kani *(Puffinus pacificus).*

Red-footed Booby *(Sula sula)*.

pacificus), Red-footed Boobies *(Sula sula)* and Brown Boobies *(Sula leucogaster)*, Brown Noddies *(Anous stolidus)*, and Sooty Terns *(Onychoprion fuscatus)*, but most likely some Masked Boobies *(Sula dactylatra)*, Black Noddies *(Anous minutes)*, and Gray-backed Terns *(Onychoprion lunatus)* are among the multitudes. In the spring and early summer, these species and others are nesting on the offshore islands. On most days during the year you can relax along this coast and watch a steady procession of year-round resident Red-footed Boobies passing close to shore as they fly toward their fishing grounds off Moloka'i. It is best to be there early in the morning.

One of the botanical highlights found at this location is coastal sandalwood or 'iliahialo'e *(Santalum ellipticum)*. These are small shrubs with roundish-shaped greenish gray leaves. The very small flowers have a sweet fragrance. Hawaiians used parts of this plant

Brown Booby
(Sula leucogaster).

Brown Noddy *(Anous stolidus)*.

Sooty Tern
(Onychoprion fuscatus).

Coastal sandalwood or 'iliahialo'e (*Santalum ellipticum*).

Akoko *(Euphorbia degeneri)*.

as an ingredient in herbal medicine to treat achy joints. If you look closely in this area, you will also find a native Hawaiian plant called akoko *(Euphorbia degeneri)*. This species is rare in the area and grows along the ground as a sprawling mat. The succulent leaves and fruits turn a blood red, which gave this plant its Hawaiian name.

Nehe *(Melanthera integrifolia)*.

Several other interesting native Hawaiian plants also occur here. The endemic nehe *(Melanthera integrifolia)* has flowers that look like little yellow daisies and are about half an inch in diameter and are either singular or in small clusters of two to three. They can be used to make beautiful leis. Nohu *(Tribulus cistoides)* is also called puncture vine because of the sharp spines on the seeds. The bright yellow flowers have five petals. The leaves are covered with microscopic hairs that prevent the surface of the leaf from drying out and help to reflect sunlight. Hawaiians used this species to treat bladder diseases and thrush.

Nohu *(Tribulus cistoides)*.

Ka'elepulu Pond–Enchanted Lake

DISTANCE: none

TIME: 1/2 hour

HIGHLIGHTS: Endangered wetland bird species and migratory and resident waterfowl.

DIRECTIONS: From Waimanalo and Kalaniana'ole Highway turn right on Keolu Drive going towards the ocean. Continue down the hill to the second left which is also Keolu Drive. Continue to Kiuke'e street and turn right. On the left side of the street you will see Ka'elepulu Pond.

NOTES: Wear sunscreen and hat. Please do not feed the birds.

DONATION AND VOLUNTEER OPPORTUNITIES:
www.kaelepuluwetland.com/

PHONE: 808-261-2179 or send an email to cindy@hotpixels.com

Ka'elepulu Pond, also known as Enchanted Lake, includes about 95 acres of water, wetlands, and several small, low islands. The water is brackish and is connected to the ocean near Kailua Beach. Before development of the Enchanted Lake subdivision in 1960, the lake covered nearly 190 acres, with an additional marsh area

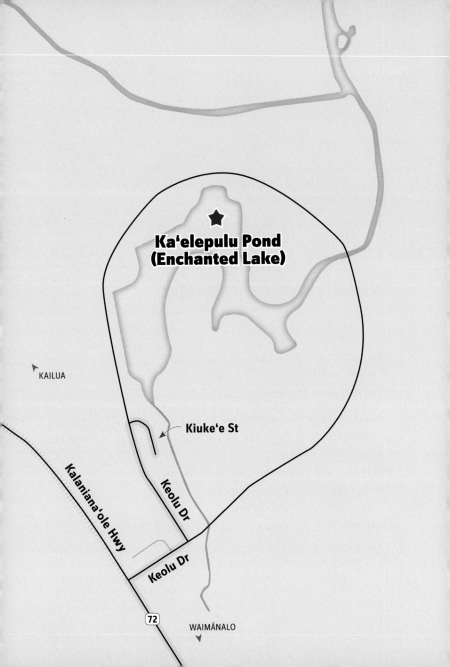

Black-necked Stilt (Himantopus mexicanus knudseni).

of 90 acres. A privately owned 5.8-acre wetland located at the southwest end of the lake was created in 1995 and was purchased by two local conservationists in August 2004. Volunteer opportunities are definitely available. This is another great area to see conservation in action on O'ahu.

This wetland is one of the best places on O'ahu to see all three endangered Hawaiian waterbirds. The Hawaiian subspecies of Black-necked Stilt *(Himantopus mexicanus knudseni)*, 'alae ke'oke'o or Hawaiian Coot *(Fulica alai)*, and 'alae 'ula, the Hawaiian subspecies of the Common Moorhen *(Gallinula chloropus)*, are all usually present. The populations of Black-necked Stilt fluctuate between 1,200 and 2,000 statewide, with as many as 600 on O'ahu. The moorhen's population is estimated at only 750 birds in Hawai'i, and the coot has the highest populations of 1,500 to 3,000 birds, with as many as 1,000 birds on O'ahu.

All three of these endangered species have declined due to severe loss of habitat and hunting, and their numbers are affected by continuing predation by rats, mongoose, housecats, dogs, and introduced bullfrogs.

'Alae ke'oke'o or Hawaiian Coot (Fulica alai).

Common Moorhen (Gallinula chloropus).

'Auku'u or Black-crowned Night-Heron
(*Nycticorax nycticorax*).

Koloa māpu or Northern Pintail
(*Anas acuta*).

Koloa mohā or Northern Shoveler
(*Anas clypeata*).

Lesser Scaup (*Aythya affinis*).

Cackling Goose (*Branta hutchinsii*).

Hybrid koloa or Hawaiian Duck
(*Anas wyvilliana*).

Black Tern *(Chlidonias niger).*

Tufted Duck *(Aythya fuligula).*

Semipalmated Plover *(Charadrius semipalmatus).*

Additional species that have been observed include the 'auku'u, or Black-crowned Night-Heron *(Nycticorax nycticorax),* koloa māpu or Northern Pintail *(Anas acuta),* koloa mohā or Northern Shoveler *(Anas clypeata),* Lesser Scaup *(Aythya affinis),* and Cackling Goose *(Branta hutchinsii).* Occasionally hybrid koloa or Hawaiian Ducks *(Anas wyvilliana)* are also present at this wetland. This species mates with Mallards, so none of the koloa on O'ahu are considered to be 100 percent pure. The U.S. Fish and Wildlife Service has warned that this threat could lead to the extinction of pure koloa if measures are not taken.

Several rare species that have been observed here include the Black Tern *(Chlidonias niger),* the Tufted Duck *(Aythya fuligula),* and the Semipalmated Plover *(Charadrius semipalmatus).*

Hāmākua Marsh Wildlife Sanctuary

DISTANCE: 1/4 mile

TIME: 1 hour

HIGHLIGHTS: Endangered wetland bird species and migratory shorebirds.

DIRECTIONS: From Honolulu take the Pali Highway to Kailua. Continue on Kalaniana'ole Highway towards Kailua which turns into Kailua Road. Turn right on Hāmākua Drive and look for Hāmākua Marsh on your right. You can park at several locations along Hāmākua Drive including behind the Down to Earth Natural Foods store.

NOTES: Please do not feed the birds and report any rare birds observed to www.oahunaturetours.com and the Hawai'i Department of Forestry and Wildlife.

DONATION AND VOLUNTEER OPPORTUNITIES:
dlnr.hawaii.gov/volunteer/ 808-587-040

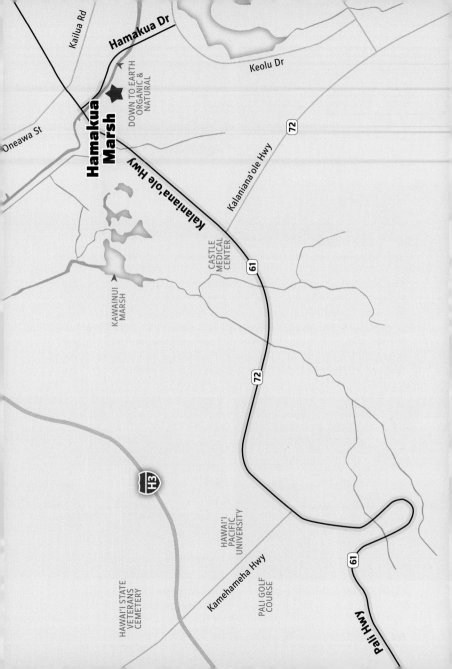

Greater Yellowlegs *(Tringa melanoleuca).*

Black-bellied Plover *(Pluvialis squatarola).*

The 22.7-acre Hāmākua Marsh Wildlife Sanctuary is conveniently located in downtown Kailua, and you can drive right to the edge of the marsh; drive-up birding at its best! It was once part of a larger wetland complex that included Kaʻelepulu Pond and Kawainui Marsh, which, at over 800 acres, is the largest remaining wetland in Hawaiʻi. Unfortunately, in the early 1960s a flood control levee was built that cut off the flow of water from Kawainui Marsh into

Lesser yellowlegs *(Tringa flavipes).*

Sharp-tailed Sandpiper *(Calidris acuminata).*

Hāmākua. As a result, Hāmākua Marsh is completely dependent on rainfall. Current and future projects intend to restore habitat and protect the native flora and fauna.

All of the endangered wetland birds that can be observed at Ka'elepulu are also found at Hāmākua. In addition, during wet years when suitable mudflats and shallow pools develop, several less common migratory shorebirds have been sighted here during the fall and winter. On March 5, 1978, the rare Greater Yellowlegs *(Tringa melanoleuca)* was recorded. A single black-bellied plover *(Pluvialis squatarola)* was seen on April 9, 2012. A lesser yellowlegs *(Tringa flavipes)* was visiting Hāmākua Marsh on November 23, 2012. The following year, the uncommon Sharp-tailed Sandpiper *(Calidris acuminata)* was documented at this location on December 29, 2013.

O'ahu has a significant number of excellent wetland areas, but as of this writing, most are unfortunately closed to the public due to a lack of visitor facilities and infrastructure caused by budgetary shortfalls. The currently closed areas include the two of the best places on O'ahu for observing migratory waterfowl and shorebirds and enjoying nature: the James Campbell National Wildlife Refuge and the Pearl Harbor National Wildlife Refuge. A bright spot on the horizon is Kawainui Marsh, which is in the process of improving and expanding wetland habitat and providing visitor opportunities.

It is hoped that these important areas will receive enough funding in the future so both residents and visitors will be able to enjoy bird-watching, photography, and environmental education, which

Long-billed Dowitcher
(Limnodromus scolopaceus).

Pectoral Sandpiper
(Calidris melanotos).

Killdeer *(Charadrius vociferous)*.

Least Sandpiper *(Calidris minutilla)*.

Dunlin *(Calidris alpina)*.

Curlew Sandpiper *(Calidris ferruginea)*.

were some of the original intended uses for our great refuge system. O'ahu is Hawai'i's most populated and visited island, but its refuges and preserves do not compare to the outer islands national wildlife refuges, which have excellent visitor centers, gift shops, infrastructure, and public access.

Because visitors and residents are currently limited to only a few wetlands on O'ahu to look for and enjoy birds, I am including the following uncommon species in the Hāmākua Marsh section,

Ruff *(Philomachus pugnax)*.   Wilson Phalarope *(Phalaropus tricolor)*.

which, to my knowledge, have never been recorded there. Some of these birds might have used the area for a limited time in the past but were missed because no one recorded them, and perhaps a few or all of these rare species will be found at Hāmākua Marsh in the future.

The habitat in the area could support Long-billed Dowitcher *(Limnodromus scolopaceus)*, Pectoral Sandpiper *(Calidris melanotos)*, Killdeer *(Charadrius vociferous)*, Least Sandpiper *(Calidris minutilla)*, Dunlin *(Calidris alpina)*, Curlew Sandpiper *(Calidris ferruginea)*, Ruff *(Philomachus pugnax)*, Wilson Phalarope *(Phalaropus tricolor)*, and Wilson Snipe *(Gallinago delicata)*. Even rarer species could be found by diligent observers. One of the greatest satisfactions of bird-watching is finding rare species, so good luck!

Wilson Snipe *(Gallinago delicata)*.

James Campbell National Wildlife Refuge

DISTANCE: 1/4 mile

TIME: 1 hour

HIGHLIGHTS: Endangered wetland bird species, migratory and resident waterfowl, shorebirds, birds of prey, seagulls, and terns.

DIRECTIONS: From Honolulu take H-1 Freeway west to Likelike Highway (Hwy. 63) then take Kahekilli (Hwy. 83) which becomes Kamehameha Highway. Turn right on Sand Road just after passing Kahuku. The refuge is closed until further notice.

NOTES: Please check if open before visiting. Wear sunscreen and hat.

DONATION AND VOLUNTEER OPPORTUNITIES: None at present.

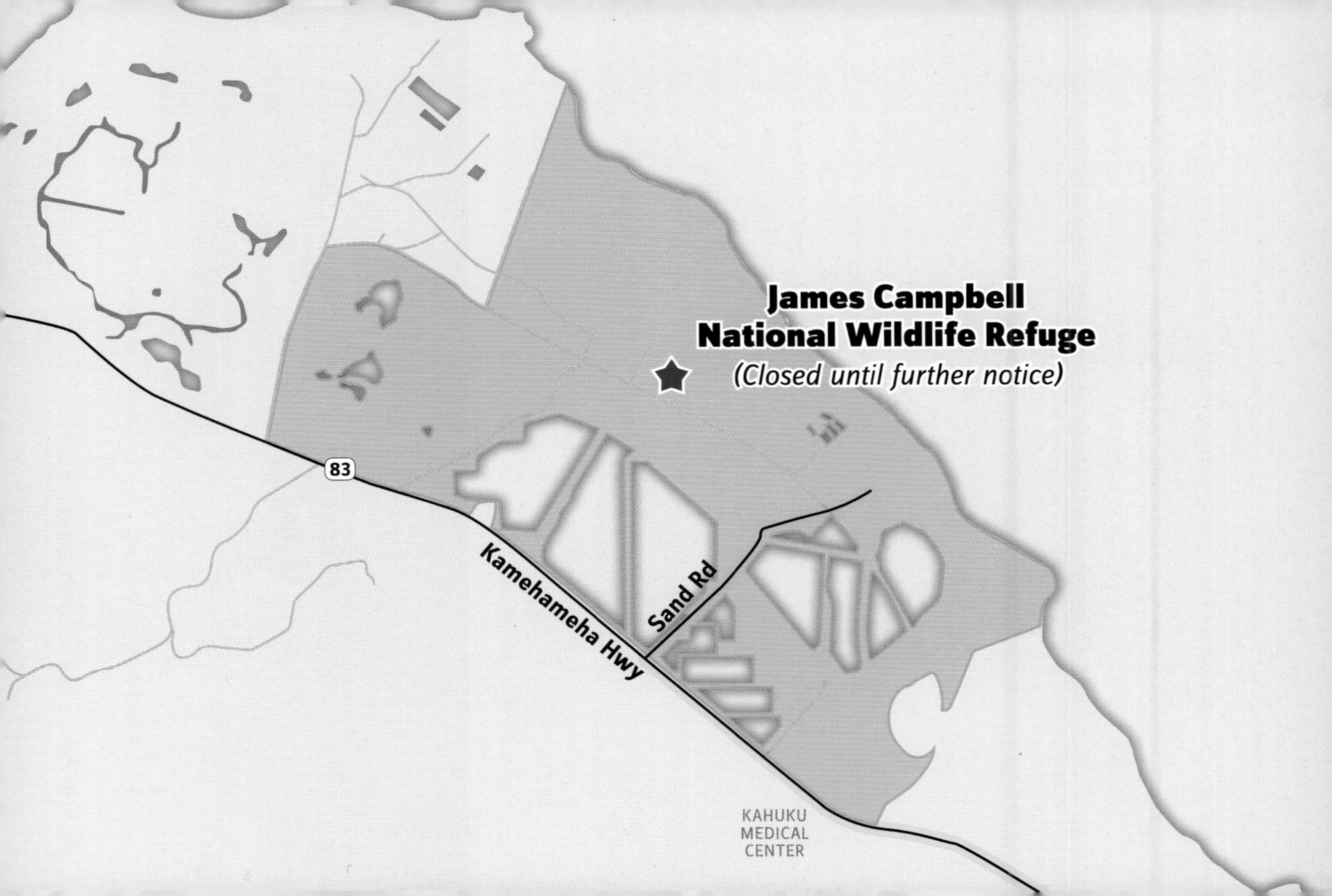

James Campbell
National Wildlife Refuge
(Closed until further notice)

Sand Rd

Kamehameha Hwy

83

KAHUKU
MEDICAL
CENTER

James Campbell National Wildlife Refuge is currently closed to the public, but I am including it as a place to enjoy nature on Oʻahu because hopefully it will reopen in the very near future once funding is secured. It is the premier wetland bird-watching location on the island. The 240-acre refuge was created in 1976 to provide habitat for endangered Hawaiian waterbirds. In 2005, the refuge expanded with the purchase of 1,100 acres to be used for providing additional habitat for endangered waterbirds, migratory waterfowl, shorebirds, seabirds, native plant species, endangered ʻīlio-holo-i-ka-uaua (Hawaiian monk seal), and threatened honu (Hawaiian green turtle).

For many years, the refuge was open to the public for several hours on Thursdays and Saturdays from October through February. Dedicated docents led visitors to a kiosk in the center of the refuge where they could view many bird species. Sadly, in 2013 these tours were canceled due to budget sequestration. Future plans call for a new visitor's center, improved walking trails, and an excellent visitor infrastructure. It is hoped that these plans will become reality soon.

More bird species have been observed on the refuge than at any other location on Oʻahu. Waterfowl species seen almost every year include the Eurasian Wigeon *(Anas Penelope)*, American Wigeon *(Anas Americana)*, Green-winged Teal *(Anas crecca)*, Ring-necked Duck *(Aythya collaris)*, and Bufflehead *(Bucephala albeola)*. Rare vagrant waterfowl species observed here include Greater White-fronted Goose *(Anser albifrons)*, Snow Goose *(Chen caerulescens)*, Brant *(Branta bernicla)*, Gadwall *(Anas strepera)*, Redhead

Eurasian Wigeon *(Anas Penelope).*

American Wigeon *(Anas Americana).*

Green-winged Teal *(Anas crecca)*.

Ring-necked Duck *(Aythya collaris)*.

Bufflehead *(Bucephala albeola)*.

Greater White-fronted Goose
(Anser albifrons).

Snow Goose *(Chen caerulescens)*.

Brant *(Branta bernicla)*.

Gadwall *(Anas strepera)*.

Redhead *(Aythya Americana)*.

Canvasback *(Aythya valisineria)*.

Hooded Merganser
(Lophodytes cucullatus).

Eared Grebe *(Podiceps nigricollis)*.

Spotted Sandpiper *(Actitis macularius)*.

(Aythya Americana), Canvasback (Aythya valisineria), Hooded Merganser (Lophodytes cucullatus), Pied-billed Grebe (Podilymbus podiceps), and Eared Grebe (Podiceps nigricollis).

Rare shorebirds seen on the refuge have included Spotted Sandpiper (Actitis macularius), Whimbrel (Numenius phaeopus), Bar-tailed Godwit (Limosa lapponica), Marbled Godwit (Limosa fedoa), Red Knot (Calidris canutus), Semipalmated Sandpiper (Calidris pusilla), and Short-billed Dowitcher (Limnodromus griseus). Extremely rare birds in Hawai'i that could be seen in this area in the future include Tundra Swan (Cygnus columbianus), Red-necked Phalarope (Phalaropus lobatus), and Common Snipe (Gallinago gallinago).

Whimbrel *(Numenius phaeopus).*

Bar-tailed Godwit *(Limosa lapponica).*

Marbled Godwit *(Limosa fedoa).*

Red Knot *(Calidris canutus).*

Semipalmated Sandpiper *(Calidris pusilla).*

Short-billed Dowitcher *(Limnodromus griseus).*

Tundra Swan *(Cygnus columbianus).*

Red-necked Phalarope
(Phalaropus lobatus).

Common Snipe *(Gallinago gallinago).*

Peregrine Falcon *(Falco peregrinus).*

Several rare birds of prey have also been observed on the refuge. These include Peregrine Falcon *(Falco peregrinus)*, Osprey *(Pandion haliaetus)*, and Northern Harrier *(Circus cyaneus)*. A Great Blue Heron *(Ardea Herodias)* was recorded at James Campbell NWR in 2006 and a White-faced Ibis *(Plegadis chihi)* in 2009. Seagulls are very rare in Hawai'i and do not breed in the state, but every year a handful of gulls arrive in Hawai'i. The refuge is a great place to look for vagrant gulls. The Laughing Gull *(Leucophaeus atricilla)* is the most likely species to be seen, followed by Franklin Gull *(Leucophaeus pipixcan)*, Bonaparte Gull *(Chroicocephalus Philadelphia)*, and Ring-billed Gull *(Larus delawarensis)*. The ponds and marshy areas are attractive

Osprey *(Pandion haliaetus)*.

Northern Harrier *(Circus cyaneus)*.

Great Blue Heron *(Ardea Herodias)*.

White-faced Ibis *(Plegadis chihi)*.

to a variety of terns that have included the Common Tern *(Sterna hirundo)*, Black Tern *(Chlidonias niger)*, and Least Tern *(Sternula antillarum)*. The Red Avadavat *(Amandava amandava)*, a beautiful introduced bird from Asia, feeds on grass seed in the area.

On September 19, 2006, I discovered a White-rumped Sandpiper *(Calidrus fuscicollis)* feeding in the mud of a drained shrimp pond on land that is now part of the refuge. This amazing bird was supposed to be spending the winter in South America after leaving its breeding areas in Northern Canada but somehow wandered many thousands of miles off course. In birding terms, this is called "vagrancy," and every fall and spring bird-watchers all over the planet

Laughing Gull *(Leucophaeus atricilla)*.

Franklin Gull *(Leucophaeus pipixcan)*.

Bonaparte Gull
(Chroicocephalus Philadelphia).

Red Avadavat *(Amandava amandava)*.

watch for any rare species that might arrive in their local area. I will never forget that special day when the rare bird I found was added to the list of Hawaiian bird species, which now numbers 332. This total does not include any species described from subfossils or any nonestablished species.

Ring-billed Gull
(*Larus delawarensis*).

Common Tern (*Sterna hirundo*).

Black Tern
(*Chlidonias niger*).

Least Tern (*Sternula antillarum*).

White-rumped
Sandpiper
(*Calidrus fuscicollis*).

Coastline North of Turtle Bay

DISTANCE: 7 miles round-trip

TIME: 4 to 5 hours

HIGHLIGHTS: Native plants, Bristle-thighed Curlew, Hawaiian monk seal, green sea turtle, excellent coastal scenery.

DIRECTIONS: From Honolulu take H-1 Freeway west to Likelike Highway (Hwy. 63) then take Kahekilli (Hwy. 83) which becomes Kamehameha Highwa. Turn right on Kuilima Drive and proceed to the public parking beach access area.

NOTES: Leave no valuables in car. Start early in the a.m. Please do not walk on native plants. Maintain adequate distance from both monk seals and green sea turtles. Wear sunscreen and hat. Do not trespass on private land above high-tide mark. Keep dogs on a leash.

DONATION AND VOLUNTEER OPPORTUNITIES: None at present.

Walking this section of the O'ahu coastline is a great way to enjoy nature on the island. It has everything: spectacular scenery, resting monk seals and green sea turtles, beautiful native coastal plants and birds, and a feeling of wildness that is difficult to find on O'ahu. It is best to park at the beach access parking lot at the Turtle Bay Resort and walk north as far as the Kakuku Golf Course and then walk back or have someone pick you up and drive back. Please be sure to use only the public beach access trails in this area. Several areas require crossing shallow waterways, so be prepared with proper shoes and so on.

Wandering Tattler *(Tringa incanus)*.

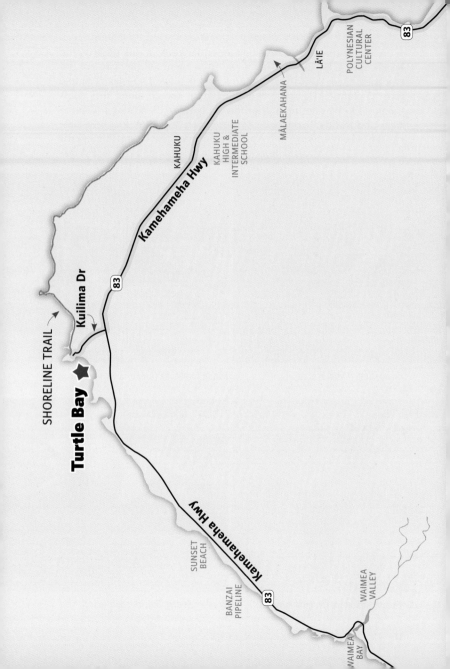

After leaving Turtle Bay, look for endangered monk seals on the beach. Please be sure to stay away from them so they can get the rest they need. At Kahuku Point, look for several species of native coastal plants. Migratory shorebirds that forage along this coast include the Wandering Tattler *(Tringa incanus)*, Sanderling *(Calidris alba)*, and Ruddy Turnstone *(Arenaria interpres)*. Look for these species between August and April. Sometimes the Great Frigatebird *(Fregata minor)*, Masked Booby *(Sula dactylatra)*, Black-footed Alba-

Sanderling *(Calidris alba)*.

Ruddy Turnstone *(Arenaria interpres)*.

Great Frigatebird *(Fregata minor)*.

Masked Booby *(Sula dactylatra)*.

tross *(Phoebastria nigripes)* and Laysan Albatross *(Phoebastria immutabilis)* can also be seen.

Watch for Ring-necked Pheasants *(Phasianus colchicus)* in the pasture areas inland from the shoreline. The best find for bird-watchers along this coast is seeing the rare Kioea or Bristle-thighed Curlew *(Numenius tahitiensis)*. The wintering flock on O'ahu varies in number

Laysan Albatross *(Phoebastria immutabilis)*.

from year to year but averages around fifty birds. Most of these are found around the ponds at James Campbell NWR, but a few visit the tide pools and beaches along this wild coast. These amazing birds fly round-trip from the Yukon to O'ahu every year.

Ring-necked Pheasant *(Phasianus colchicus)*.

Kioea or Bristle-thighed Curlew *(Numenius tahitiensis)*.

Ka'ena Point State Park and Natural Area Reserve

DISTANCE: 6 miles round-trip

TIME: Minimum 3 to 4 hours

HIGHLIGHTS: Laysan Albatross (November to July), humpback whales (November to April), monk seals, native plants, excellent coastal scenery.

DIRECTIONS: Take H-2 to Kaukonahua Road (Route 803) to Farrington Highway (Route 930) past Waialua and go about 1 mile past Camp Erdman. The trailhead to Ka'ena Point begins where the paved road ends and a rough four-wheel-drive road begins.

NOTES: Bring plenty of water, leave no valuables in car, start early in the a.m. Do not disturb birds or leave trails inside the reserve. Please clean footwear before hike and before entering reserve; best to leave dogs at home. Bring cellular phone and sunscreen.

DONATION AND VOLUNTEER OPPORTUNITIES: Please contact Friends of Ka'ena at www.friendsofkaena.org/join-us.

Ka'ena Point State Park and Natural Area Reserve at the very tip of the point is one of the best places to experience nature on O'ahu. The narrow strip of land and shoreline that lies just below the towering cliffs of the ancient Wai'anae Volcano is one of the island's most rugged and best-preserved coastal areas. It is also an excellent location to see conservation in action. The trail begins at the parking area where the road ends. You will see many large black lava rocks. Be sure to leave nothing of value in the car and leave nothing on the seats that might be perceived as valuables.

The trail is a dirt road that is used by four-wheel-drive (4WDR) vehicles; do not drive a non-4WDR on this road. If you have a 4WDR, be very careful if it has rained, as many 4WDR vehicles get stuck. 4WDR owners will need a permit from the DNLR to drive past the locked gate. There are several trails/roads in the area. The main one is the dirt road inland from and parallel to the coast. Some minor trails/roads that spur off the main road will take you closer to the ocean.

In the Hawaiian language, Ka'ena means "the heat" and is a reference to either a brother or cousin of Pele, the Hawaiian volcano goddess. Several archaeological sites have been discovered in the

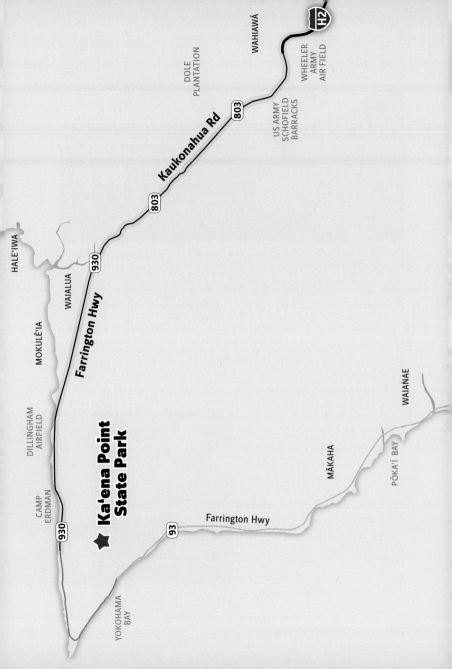

The trail is a dirt road that is used by four-wheel-drive (4WDR) vehicles; do not drive a non–4WDR on this road.

area. This location is considered very sacred to the Hawaiian people because they believe the large rock near the end of the point, Leina-a-ka-ʻuhane ("leap of the soul"), is where souls lept to the netherworld.

Just offshore of the very end of the point is a rock called Pōhaku o Kauaʻi, which according to tradition was once a part of Kauaʻi. The boulder was brought to Oʻahu when Māui, the Hawaiian superhero demigod, attempted to bring Kauaʻi closer to Oʻahu. Māui used his supernatural hook, Manaʻia-ka-lani, to snag Kauaʻi and pull it closer to Oʻahu. During this effort, a part of Kauaʻi—Pōhahu o Kauaʻi—suddenly broke off and catapulted to the tip of Kaʻena Point.[32] This is the extreme westernmost place on Oʻahu.

For many years, livestock was grazed in this area. Walter Dillingham's Oʻahu Railroad and Land Company built a railroad line around Kaʻena Point in

ʻŌhelo kai *(Lysium sandwicense).*

'Ilima *(Sida fallax)*.

1898. The tracks were damaged by the 1946 tsunami, and service ended the following year.

One of the most conspicuous small trees you see along the road/trail (closest to the mountains) is the sweet-smelling naio *(Myoporum sandwicense)*. Look for the small white flowers and enjoy the fragrance. Native Hawaiians used the wood to make house posts, gunwales for their outrigger canoes, and torches for nighttime fishing. This tree is known as "bastard sandalwood" because it was used as a poor substitute to replace the valuable and aromatic sandalwood trees that were quickly depleted by 1840 in Hawai'i due to overexploitation. Naio wood was occasionally sent to the Chinese merchants instead of sandalwood, but they rejected this species.

If you walk toward the ocean on the way out to the point, you will see the elevated coral reef limestone. A beautiful species of native coastal plant grows here called 'ōhelo kai *(Lysium sandwicense)*. Look for the succulent leaves and the bright red fruit. The golden orange-flowered 'ilima *(Sida fallax)*, the official flower of O'ahu, grows in colorful mats between the limestone reef and the dirt trail. Thousands of the tiny flowers are used to make a single lei. Hawaiians used this plant in combination with other species to treat

Pā'ū-o-Hi'iaka *(Jacquemontia ovalifolia)*.

Humpback whale *(Megaptera novaeangliae)*.

Erckel Francolin *(Francolinus erckelii)*.

Black Francolin *(Francolinus francolinus)*.

asthma, constipation, and to help ease the pain of childbirth. In some areas near the coast you will see a tiny, pale blue–flowered vine. This is pāʻū-o-Hiʻiaka *(Jacquemontia ovalifolia)*. The Hawaiian name means "skirt of Hiʻiaka" and is derived from a legend that tells how Hiʻiaka, the younger sister of Pele, was sleeping on the beach and this plant grew around her to protect her from the burning sun.

While walking to and from the point between November and April, it is a good idea to stop occasionally to look for humpback whales *(Megaptera novaeangliae)*. Sometimes you might see them spouting, tail or fin flapping, or the most spectacular of all—a breach. Adults can weigh 80,000 pounds and measure more than 50 feet long, so they make a huge splash. Watch for small grouse-size brown birds feeding near the brush or perhaps in the open. Most likely these are Gray Francolin, which are native to the Middle East and India. They were first recorded on Oʻahu in 1980. Two other game bird species, Erckel Francolin *(Francolinus erckelii)* and the Black Francolin *(Francolinus francolinus),* have been observed at Kaʻena but are less common.

As you approach the end of the State Park, you will see this sign and large boulders

Recently constructed predator-proof fence.

that mark the entrance to the Natural Area Reserve. Here you will find the recently constructed predator-proof fence that includes two double-door entry gates. Be sure to clean your shoes so no weedy seeds are carried into the reserve area. It's a good idea to do this before you begin your walk and also here.

Once you pass through these gates, you have entered the reserve and the best location on Oʻahu for observing native Hawaiian coastal plants. Some areas are completely weed free, and you can enjoy the perfection of nature's floral creations. One of the most beautiful is the ʻōhai *(Sesbania tomentosa),* which has stunning red-orange flowers. In 2003, the U.S. Fish and Wildlife Service designated critical habitat areas for this species after

ʻŌhai *(Sesbania tomentosa).*

Laysan Albatross, or mōlī *(Phoebastria immutabilis)*.

Northern Mockingbird *(Mimus polyglottos)*.

only fifty-five individual plants in three occurrences were known to be left on O'ahu.

If you visit between November and July, you most likely will see the magnificent Laysan Albatross, or mōlī in Hawaiian (*Phoebastria immutabilis*), flying very close as they glide effortlessly on huge wings. This is the only accessible Laysan Albatross colony on O'ahu. These incredible birds can live to be over sixty-five years old and sometimes fly thousands of miles to Alaska from Ka'ena Point in order to bring food back to their growing chicks.

The work being done at Ka'ena Point is one of O'ahu's best examples of conservation to save and restore Hawai'i's native flora and fauna. The 2,000-foot fence protects 59 acres of land and was completed in March 2011. In 2006, dogs killed twenty-one Wedge-tailed Shearwater chicks in a single night at Ka'ena Point. One evening in 2007, more than 125 native seabirds were killed, most likely by one or more dogs. Rats kill and eat nestling chicks, and they also eat seeds of native plants, preventing the growth and spread of new plants.

Once the fence was finished, intensive efforts began to remove predatory animals from the reserve by using traps for larger animals and bait boxes for rodents. In 2012, sixty-two pairs of Laysan Albatross were present, compared to no pairs in 1989. The Wedge-tailed Shearwaters at Ka'ena Point are also starting to increase, as are the native plants.

At the very tip of the point, look for the sign and then see if you can locate a monk seal (*Monachus schauinslandi*) at rest on the sand and rocks below. Please stay 50 yards away from resting seals so you do not disturb them.

Look for this "Hawaiian Monk Seal" sign at the tip of Ka'ena Point.

Brown boobies *(Sula leucogaster)* can be seen along this coast, and Ka'ena Point is one of the best places on O'ahu to see the introduced Northern Mockingbird *(Mimus polyglottos)*. Watch for the elegant White-tailed Tropicbird or koa'e kea *(Phaethon lepturus)* riding the warm air thermals above the cliffs. These graceful flyers are rare on O'ahu and are the smallest of the world's three Tropicbird species.

White-tailed Tropicbird or koa'e kea *(Phaethon lepturus).*

While visiting Ka'ena Point you might observe a rare seagull, and please report any sightings to O'ahu Nature Tours at www.oahunaturetours.com or to Friends of Ka'ena at the above website. On December 27, 2009, a Glaucous-winged Gull *(Larus glaucescens)* was photographed in the area. This was one of only ninety-six sightings of this species in the southern Hawaiian islands ever recorded. An even rarer species, the Black-legged Kittiwake *(Rissa tridactyla),* with only five historical records in

Glaucous-winged Gull *(Larus glaucescens).*

Hawai'i, was reported in the vicinity of Ka'ena Point on February 11, 2012. Seagulls do not breed in the islands and are considered rare.

Checklist of All Bird Species Recorded on O'ahu

Does not include non-established species or species known only from sub-fossils.

Extinct species bold red

African Silverbill	
'Akepa	
'Amaui	
American Wigeon	
Ancient Murrelet	
'Apapane	
Arctic Tern	
Baird Sandpiper	
Band-rumped Storm-Petrel	
Barn Owl	
Bar-tailed Godwit	
Belted Kingfisher	
Black Francolin	
Black Noddy	
Black Tern	
Black-bellied Plover	
Black-crowned Night-Heron	
Black-footed Albatross	
Black-headed Gull	
Black-legged Kittiwake	
Black-necked Stilt	
Black-tailed Godwit	
Black-winged Petrel	

Blue-winged Teal	
Bonaparte Gull	
Bonin Petrel	
Brant	
Bristle-thighed Curlew	
Brown Booby	
Brown Noddy	
Buff-breasted Sandpiper	
Bufflehead	
Buller Shearwater	
Bulwer Petrel	
Cackling Goose	
California Gull	
California Quail	
Canada Goose	
Canvasback	
Caspian Tern	
Cattle Egret	
Chestnut Munia	
Christmas Shearwater	
Chukar	
Cinnamon Teal	
Common Merganser	

	Common Moorhen		Greater White-fronted Goose
	Common Myna		Greater Yellowlegs
	Common Peafowl		Green Heron
	Common Snipe		Green-winged Teal
	Common Tern		Gull-billed Tern
	Common Waxbill		Hawaiian Coot
	Cook Petrel		Hawaiian Duck
	Curlew Sandpiper		Hawaiian Goose
	Dunlin		Hawaiian Petrel
	Eared Grebe		Herring Gull
	'Elepaio		Hooded Merganser
	Emperor Goose		House Finch
	Erckel Francolin		House Sparrow
	Eurasian Wigeon		Hudsonian Godwit
	Franklin Gull		Hwamei
	Gadwall		'I'iwi
	Garganey		Japanese Bush-Warbler
	Glaucous Gull		Japanese Quail
	Glaucous-winged Gull		Japanese White-eye
	Gray Francolin		Java Sparrow
	Gray-backed Tern		Juan Fernandez Petrel
	Gray-sided Laughingthrush		Kermadec Petrel
	Gray-tailed Tattler		Killdeer
	Great Blue Heron		Laughing Gull
	Great Crested Tern		Lavender Waxbill
	Great Egret		Laysan Albatross
	Great Frigatebird		Leach Storm-Petrel
	Greater 'Akialoa		Least Sandpiper
	Greater Scaup		Least Tern

	Lesser Frigatebird
	Lesser Scaup
	Lesser Yellowlegs
	Little Blue Heron
	Little Stint
	Long-billed Dowitcher
	Long-tailed Duck
	Long-tailed Jaeger
	Mallard
	Marbled Godwit
	Mariana Swiftlet
	Marsh Sandpiper
	Masked Booby
	Merlin
	Mottled Petrel
	Mourning Dove
	Murphy Petrel
	Nazca Booby
	Newell Shearwater
	Northern Cardinal
	Northern Fulmar
	Northern Harrier
	Northern Mockingbird
	Northern Pintail
	Northern Shoveler
	Nukupuu
	Nutmeg Mannikin
	O'ahu 'Alauahio
	O'ahu 'Amakihi

	Oahu 'O'o
	Orange-cheeked Waxbill
	Osprey
	'O'u
	Pacific Golden-Plover
	Pacific Loon
	Parasitic Jaeger
	Pectoral Sandpiper
	Peregrine Falcon
	Pied-billed Grebe
	Pomarine Jaeger
	Red Avadavat
	Red Junglefowl
	Red Knot
	Red Phalarope
	Red-billed Leiothrix
	Red-billed Tropicbird
	Red-breasted Merganser
	Red-crested Cardinal
	Red-crowned Parrot
	Red-footed Booby
	Redhead
	Red-masked Parakeet
	Red-necked Phalarope
	Red-necked Stint
	Red-tailed Tropicbird
	Red-vented Bulbul
	Red-whiskered Bulbul
	Ring-billed Gull

☐	Ring-necked Duck	☐	Spotted Dove
☐	Ring-necked Pheasant	☐	Spotted Sandpiper
☐	Rock Pigeon	☐	Stejneger Petrel
☐	Rose-ringed Parakeet	☐	Stilt Sandpiper
☐	Ruddy Duck	☐	Surdfbird
☐	Ruddy Turnstone	☐	Surf Scoter
☐	Ruff	☐	Terek Sandpiper
☐	Saffron Finch	☐	Tufted Duck
☐	Sanderling	☐	Varied Tit
☐	Sandhill Crane	☐	Wandering Tattler
☐	Sandwich Tern	☐	Wedge-tailed Shearwater
☐	Semipalmated Plover	☐	Western Gull
☐	Semipalmated Sandpiper	☐	Western Sandpiper
☐	Sharp-tailed Sandpiper	☐	Whimbrel
☐	Short-billed Dowitcher	☐	White Tern
☐	Short-eared Owl	☐	White-faced Ibis
☐	Short-tailed Shearwater	☐	White-rumped Sandpiper
☐	Sky Lark	☐	White-rumped Shama
☐	Slaty-backed Gull	☐	White-tailed Tropicbird
☐	Snow Goose	☐	Wild Turkey
☐	Snowy Egret	☐	Willet
☐	Solitary Sandpiper	☐	Wilson Phalarope
☐	Sooty Shearwater	☐	Wilson Snipe
☐	Sooty Tern	☐	Yellow-faced Grassquit
☐	Sora	☐	Yellow-fronted Canary
☐	South Polar Skua	☐	Zebra Dove

Endnotes

1. Sinton, J. M., D. E. Eason, M. Tardona, D. Pyle, I. van der Zander, H. Guillou, D. Clague, and J. J. Mahoney. 2014. "Kaʻena Volcano: A Precursor Volcano of the Island of Oʻahu, Hawaiʻi. *Geological Society of America Bulletin.* Published online May 2.

2. Pukui, Mary K. and Elbert, Samuel H. *Hawaiian Dictionary.* Honolulu: Universtiy of Hawaii Press, 1986 .

3. MacDonald, Gordon Andrew. 1983. *Volcanoes in the Sea: The Geology of Hawaii.* Honolulu: University of Hawaiʻi Press.

4. Moore, J. G. 1964. "Giant Submarine Landslides on the Hawaiian Ridge." *U.S. Geological Survey Professional Paper* 501-D

5 Ruhe, R. V., J. M. Williams, and E. L. Hill. 1965. "Shorelines and Submarine Shelves, Oahu, Hawaii." *Journal of Geology* 73(3): 485–497.

6. MacDonald, Gordon Andrew. 1983. *Volcanoes in the Sea: The Geology of Hawaii.* Honolulu: University of Hawaiʻi Press.

7. "Ibid.,"

8. Juvik, Sonia P., and James O. Juvik, eds. 1998. *Atlas of Hawaiʻi.* 3rd ed. Honolulu: University of Hawaiʻi Press.

9. "Ibid.,"

10. Carlquist, S. 1970. *Hawaii: A Natural History.* New York: Natural History Press.

11. Wagner, W. L., D. R. Herbst, and S. H. Sohmer. 1999. *Manual of the Flowering Plants of Hawaiʻi.* Rev. ed. 2 vols. Bishop Museum Special Publication 97. Honolulu: University of Hawaiʻi Press and Bishop Museum Press.

12. Givnish, Thomas J., Kendra C. Millam, Austin R. Mast, Thomas B. Paterson, Terra J. Theim, Andrew L. Hipp, Jillian M. Henss, James F. Smith, Kenneth R. Wood, and Kenneth J. Sytsma. 2009. "Origin, Adaptive Radiation and Diversification of the Hawaiian Lobeliads *(Asterales: Campanulaceae)*." In *Proceedings of the Royal Society: Biological Sciences,* n.p.

13. Lerner, Heather R. L., Matthias Meyer, Helen F. James, Michael Hofreiter, and Robert C. Fleischer. 2011. "Multilocus Resolution of Phylogeny and Timescale in the Extant Adaptive Radiation of Hawaiian HoneyCreepers." *Current Biology* 21 (November 8): 1–7.

14. Pratt, H. D. 2005. *The Hawaiian HoneyCreepers:* Drepanidinae. Series: Bird Families of the World. Oxford: Oxford University Press

15. Kirch, Patrick V. 2011. "When Did the Polynesians Settle Hawaiʻi? A Review of 150 Years of Scholarly Inquiry and a Tentative Answer." *Hawaiian Archaeology* 12: 3–26.

16. Kirch, Patrick V. 1985. *Feathered Gods and Fishhooks: An Introduction to Hawaiian Archaeology and Prehistory.* Honolulu: University of Hawaiʻi Press.

17. Athens, J. Stephen. 2009. "Rattus exulans and the Catastrophic Disappearance of Hawaiʻiʻs Native Lowland Forest." *Biological Invasions* 11(7): 1489–1501.

18. James C. Beaglehole, *The Journals of Captain James Cook On His Voyages of Discovery,* vol. 3, part 1 (Cambridge: Cambridge UP, 1967) 569.

19. Portlock, Nathaniel. A Voyage Round the World; But More Particularly to the North-West Coast of America; Performed in 1785, 1786, 1787, and 1788, in the King George and Queen Charlotte, Captains Portlock and Dixon. Embellished with Twenty Copper-Plates. Dedicated, by Permission, to His Majesty. By Captain Nathaniel Portlock. (London: Printed for John Stockdale; and George Goulding, 1789).

20. Athens, J. Stephen 1997 *Hawaiian native lowland vegetation in prehistory.* In Historical Ecology in the Pacific Islands, ed. by Patrick V. Kirch and Terry L. Hunt, pp. 248-270. Yale University Press, Connecticut

21. Athens, J. S., J. V. Ward, and S. Wickler. 1992. "Late Holocene Lowland Vegetation, Oʻahu, Hawaiʻi." *New Zealand Journal of Archaeology* 14: 9–34.

22. Olson, Storrs L. 1982. *Prodromus of the Fossil Avifauna of the Hawaiian Islands. Smithsonian Contributions to Zoology* 365: 1–59.

23. Olson, Storrs L., and Helen F. James. 2004. "Fossil Birds from the Hawaiian Islands: Evidence for Wholesale Extinction by Man before Western Contact" [reprint of Science 217:633-35]. In D. Lomolino, F. Sax, and J. H. Brown, eds., *Foundations of Biogeography: Classic Papers with Commentaries* (Chicago and London: University of Chicago Press), 1023–1025.

24.———. 1989. "The Role of Polynesians in the Extinction of the Avifauna of the Hawaiian Islands." In Paul S. Martin and Richard G. Klein, eds., *Quaternary Extinctions: A Prehistoric Revolution* (Tucson: University of Arizona Press), 768–780.

25. Tomich, P. Q. 1986. *Mammals in Hawaiʻi.* 2nd ed. Honolulu: Bishop Museum Press.

26. Pyle, R. L., and P. Pyle. 2009. *The Birds of the Hawaiian Islands: Occurrence, History, Distribution, and Status.* Honolulu: B. P. Bishop Museum. Version 1 (December 31, 2009). Available at hbs.bishopmuseum.org/birds/rlp-monograph.

27. VanderWerf, E. A., J. L. Rohrer, D. G. Smith, and M. D. Burt. 2001. "Current Distribution and Abundance of the Oʻahu ʻElepaio." *Wilson Bulletin* 113: 10–16 (reprinted in *ʻElepaio* 61: 55–61).

28. Shallenberger, R. J., and H. D. Pratt. 1978. "Recent Observations and Field Identification of the Oahu Creeper." *ʻElepaio* 38: 135–140.

29. Pyle, R. L., and P. Pyle. 2009. *The Birds of the Hawaiian Islands*

30. MacDonald, Gordon Andrew. 1983. *Volcanoes in the Sea.*

31. "Ibid.,"

32. Westervelt, W. D. *Legends of gods and ghosts : (Hawaiian mythology) collected and tr. from the Hawaiian* Ellis Press Boston 1915

Bibliography

Athens, J. Stephen. 1997. "Hawaiian Native Lowland Vegetation in Prehistory." In *Historical Ecology in the Pacific Islands*, ed. by Patrick V. Kirch and Terry L. Hunt (New Haven, CT: Yale University Press), 248–270.

———. 2009. "Rattus exulans and the Catastrophic Disappearance of Hawai'i's Native Lowland Forest." *Biological Invasions* 11(7): 1489–1501.

Athens, J. Stephen, and Jerome V. Ward. 1993. "Environmental Change and Prehistoric Polynesian Settlement in Hawai'i." *Asian Perspectives* 32(2): 205–223.

Athens, J. S., J. V. Ward, and S. Wickler. 1992. "Late Holocene Lowland Vegetation, O'ahu, Hawai'i." *New Zealand Journal of Archaeology* 14: 9–34.

Atkinson, C. T., K. L. Woods, D. L. Dusek, L. S. Sileo, and W. M. Iko. 1995. "Wildlife Disease and Conservation in Hawaii: Pathogenicity of Avian Malaria *(Plasmodium relictum)* in Experimentally Infected Iiwi *(Vestiaria coccinea)*." *Parasitology* 111: S59–S69.

Atkinson, I. A. E. 1977. "A Reassessment of Factors, Particularly *Rattus rattus* L., That Influenced the Decline of Endemic Forest Birds in the Hawaiian Islands." *Pacific Science* 31: 109–133.

Beaglehole, James C., *The Journals of Captain James Cook On His Voyages of Discovery,* vol. 3, part 1 (Cambridge: Cambridge UP, 1967) 569.

Carlquist, S. 1970. *Hawaii: A Natural History*. New York: Natural History Press.

Conant, S., C. C. Christensen, P. Conant, W. C. Gagné, and M. L. Goff. 1994. "The Unique Terrestrial Biota of the Northwestern Hawaiian Islands." In *A Natural History of the Hawaiian Islands: Selected Readings II* (Honolulu: University of Hawai'i Press), 378–390.

Cook, J., and J. King. 1784. *A Voyage to the Pacific Ocean Performed in His Majesty's Ships Resolution and Discovery in the years 1776, 1777, 1778, 1779, 1780.* Vol. 2. G. London: Nicol and T. Cadell.

Cuddihy, L. W., and C. P. Stone. 1990. *Alteration of Native Hawaiian Vegetation: Effects of Humans, Their Activities and Introductions.* Honolulu: University of Hawai'i Cooperative National Park Resources Studies Unit.

Dalrymple, G. B., D. A. Clague, and M. A. Lanphere. 1977. "Revised Age for Midway Volcano, Hawaiian Volcanic Chain." *Earth and Planetary Science Letters* 37: 107–116.

Department of Business, Economic Development, and Tourism. 2013. *The State of Hawaii Data Book: 2013.* Available at dbedt.hawaii.gov/.

Dixon, G. 1789. *A Voyage around the World; but More Particularly to the North-West Coast of America: Performed in 1785, 1786, 1787, and 1788, in the King George and Queen Charlotte, Captains Portlock and Dixon.* London: Geo. Goulding.

Fleischer, Robert C., Storrs L. Olson, Helen F. James, and A. C. Cooper. 2000. "Identification of the Extinct Hawaiian Eagle *(Haliaeetus)* by Mitochondrial DNA Sequence." *The Auk* 117(4): 1051–1056.

Fryer, Gerard. www.soest.hawaii.edu/GG/ASK/oahu-quakes2.html. Hawaii Institute of Geophysics and Planetology, University of Hawai'i, Honolulu.

Garcia, M., and J. M. Stinton. 1979. *Field Trip Guide to the Hawaiian Islands, Oahu and Maui.* Hawai'i Institute of Geophysics Special Publication 1.

Givnish, Thomas J., Kendra C. Millam, Austin R. Mast, Thomas B. Paterson, Terra J. Theim, Andrew L. Hipp, Jillian M. Henss, James F. Smith, Kenneth R. Wood, and Kenneth J. Sytsma. 2009. "Origin, Adaptive Radiation and Diversification of the Hawaiian Lobeliads *(Asterales: Campanulaceae)*." In *Proceedings of the Royal Society: Biological Sciences*, n.p.

James, H. F. 1987. "A Late Pleistocene Avifauna from the Island of Oahu, Hawaiian Islands." *Documents Labs. Geol. de Lyon* 99:121–128.

James, H. F., and S. L. Olson. 1991. "Descriptions of 32 New Species of Hawaiian Birds. Part II: Passeriformes." *Ornithological Monographs* 46: 1–88.

Juvik, Sonia P., and James O. Juvik, eds. 1998. *Atlas of Hawai'i.* 3rd ed. Honolulu: University of Hawai'i Press.

Kirch, Patrick V. 1985. *Feathered Gods and Fishhooks: An Introduction to Hawaiian Archaeology and Prehistory.* Honolulu: University of Hawai'i Press.

———. 2011. "When Did the Polynesians Settle Hawai'i? A Review of 150 Years of Scholarly Inquiry and a Tentative Answer." *Hawaiian Archaeology* 12: 3–26.

Kirch, Patrick V., and Terry L. Hunt, eds. 1997. *Historical Ecology in the Pacific Islands: Prehistoric Environmental and Landscape Change.* New Haven, CT: Yale University Press.

Lerner, Heather R. L., Matthias Meyer, Helen F. James, Michael Hofreiter, and Robert C. Fleischer. 2011. "Multilocus Resolution of Phylogeny and Timescale in the Extant Adaptive Radiation of Hawaiian HoneyCreepers." *Current Biology* 21 (November 8): 1–7.

MacDonald, Gordon Andrew. 1983. *Volcanoes in the Sea: The Geology of Hawaii.* Honolulu: University of Hawai'i Press.

Moore, J. G. 1964. "Giant Submarine Landslides on the Hawaiian Ridge." *U.S. Geological Survey Professional Paper* 501-D: 95–98.

Olson, Storrs L. 1982. *Prodromus of the Fossil Avifauna of the Hawaiian Islands. Smithsonian Contributions to Zoology* 365: 1–59.

Olson, Storrs L., and Helen F. James. 2004. "Fossil Birds from the Hawaiian Islands: Evidence for Wholesale Extinction by Man before Western Contact" [reprint of Science 217:633-35]. In D. Lomolino, F. Sax, and J. H. Brown, eds., *Foundations of Biogeography: Classic Papers with Commentaries* (Chicago and London: University of Chicago Press), 1023–1025.

———. 1989. "The Role of Polynesians in the Extinction of the Avifauna of the Hawaiian Islands." In Paul S. Martin and Richard G. Klein, eds., *Quaternary Extinctions: A Prehistoric Revolution* (Tucson: University of Arizona Press), 768–780.

Pararas-Carayannis, George. 1969. *Catalog of Tsunamis in the Hawaiian Islands.* World Data Center A—Tsunami U.S. Dept. of Commerce Environmental Science Service Administration Coast and Geodetic Survey, May.

Pearson, Richard J., Patrick Vinton Kirch, and Michael Pietrusewsky. 1971. "An

Early Prehistoric Site at Bellows Beach, Waimanalo, Oahu, Hawaiian Islands." *Archaeology and Physical Anthropology in Oceania* 6(3): 204–234.

Pemberton, C. E. 1964. "Highlights in the History of Entomolgy in the Hawaiian Islands 17781963." *Pacific Insects* 6(4): 689–729.

Portlock, Nathaniel. A Voyage Round the World; But More Particularly to the North-West Coast of America; Performed in 1785, 1786, 1787, and 1788, in the King George and Queen Charlotte, Captains Portlock and Dixon. Embellished with Twenty Copper-Plates. Dedicated, by Permission, to His Majesty. By Captain Nathaniel Portlock. (London: Printed for John Stockdale; and George Goulding, 1789).

Pratt, H. D. 2005. *The Hawaiian HoneyCreepers:* Drepanidinae. Series: Bird Families of the World. Oxford: Oxford University Press.

Pyle, R. L., and P. Pyle. 2009. *The Birds of the Hawaiian Islands: Occurrence, History, Distribution, and Status.* Honolulu: B. P. Bishop Museum. Version 1 (December 31, 2009). Available at hbs.bishopmuseum.org/birds/rlp-monograph.

Pukui, Mary K. and Elbert, Samuel H. *Hawaiian Dictionary.* Honolulu: Universtiy of Hawaii Press, 1986.

Ruhe, R. V., J. M. Williams, and E. L. Hill. 1965. "Shorelines and Submarine Shelves, Oahu, Hawaii." *Journal of Geology* 73(3): 485–497.

Scott, Susan. 1991. *Plants and Animals of Hawai'i.* Honolulu: Bess Press.

Shallenberger, R. J., and H. D. Pratt. 1978. "Recent Observations and Field Identification of the Oahu Creeper." *'Elepaio* 38: 135–140.

Sinton, J. M., D. E. Eason, M. Tardona, D. Pyle, I. van der Zander, H. Guillou, D. Clague, and J. J. Mahoney. 2014. "Ka'ena Volcano: A Precursor Volcano of the Island of O'ahu, Hawai'i. *Geological Society of America Bulletin.* Published online May 2.

Tomich, P. Q. 1986. *Mammals in Hawai'i.* 2nd ed. Honolulu: Bishop Museum Press.

Twain, Mark. 1866. "Scenes in Honolulu #4." Sacramento Union Newspaper, April 19.

U.S. Department of the Interior, U.S. Geological Survey. URL: volcanoes.usgs.gov/hazards/gas/index.php.

VanderWerf, E. A., and J. L. Rohrer. 1996. "Discovery of an 'I'iwi Population in the Ko'olau Mountains of O'ahu." *'Elepaio* 56: 25–28.

VanderWerf, E. A., J. L. Rohrer, D. G. Smith, and M. D. Burt. 2001. "Current Distribution and Abundance of the O'ahu 'Elepaio." *Wilson Bulletin* 113: 10–16 (reprinted in *'Elepaio* 61: 55–61).

Wagner, W. L., D. R. Herbst, and S. H. Sohmer. 1999. *Manual of the Flowering Plants of Hawai'i.* Rev. ed. 2 vols. Bishop Museum Special Publication 97. Honolulu: University of Hawai'i Press and Bishop Museum Press.

Westervelt, W. D. *Legends of gods and ghosts : (Hawaiian mythology) collected and tr. from the Hawaiian* Ellis Press Boston 1915

Ziegler, A. C. 2002. *Hawaiian Natural History, Ecology, and Evolution.* Honolulu: University of Hawai'i Press.

Recommended Books

The following guide books will help you identify the flora and fauna on Oʻahu and learn more about the island environment.

Field Guide to Birds of Hawaiʻi and the Tropical Pacific
by H. Douglas Pratt

A Guide to Hawaiʻi's Coastal Plants
by Michael Walther

Hawaiian Insects and their Kin
by Francis G. Howarth
and William P. Mull

Hawaiʻi's Beautiful Birds
by H. Douglas Pratt

Hawaii's Birds
by Hawaii Audubon Society

*Hawaiʻi's Fishes:
A Guide for Snorkelers and Divers*
by John P. Hoover

Hawaiʻi's Native Plants
by Dr. Bruce A. Bohm

*A Hiker's Guide to
Trailside Plants in Hawaiʻi*
by John B. Hall

Mammals in Hawaiʻi
by P. Quentin Tomich

Manual of the Flowering Plants of Hawaiʻi by Warren L. Wagner, Derral R. Herbst, and S. H. Sohmer

A Photographic Guide to the Birds of Hawaiʻi: The Main Islands and Offshore Waters by Jim Denny

A Pocket Guide to Hawaiʻi's Birds and Their Habitats
by H. Douglas Pratt

*A Pocket Guide to
Hawaiʻi's Trees and Shrubs*
by H. Douglas Pratt

*A Pocket Guide to
Hawaiʻi's Wildlife*
by H. Douglas Pratt

Sea Turtles: An Ecological Guide
by David Gulko
and Karen Eckert

O'ahu Environmental Nonprofits

'Ahahui Mālama I Ka Lōkahi:
Hawaiians for the Conservation of
Native Ecosystems
www.ahahui.net

American Bird Conservancy
www.abcbirds.org
1 (888) 247-3624

Beach Environmental Awareness
Campaign Hawaii
www.b-e-a-c-h.org

Bernice Pauahi Bishop Museum
www.bishopmuseum.org
(808) 847-3511

Friends of Hanauma Bay
www.friendsofhanaumabay.org

Friends of Ka'ena
www.friendsofkaena.org

Hawai'i Association of Watershed
Partnerships
hawp.org/category/news/volunteer-
opportunities

Hawaii Audubon Society
www.hawaiiaudubon.org
(808) 528-1432

Hawai'i Nature Center
www.hawaiinaturecenter.org
(808) 955-0100

Hawai'i Conservation Alliance
www.hawaiiconservation.org

Hawai'i Wildlife Fund
wildhawaii.org/index.html
(808) 280-8124

Hui o Ko'olaupoko: Protecting
ocean health by restoring the 'āina
mauka to makai
www.huihawaii.org
(808) 277-5611

Livable Hawaii Kai Hui
www.old.hawaiikaihui.org/4436.html

Lyon Arboretum
www.hawaii.edu/lyonarboretum
(808) 988-0456

Mālama na Honu
www.malamanahonu.org

Mānoa Cliff Trail Project
manoacliffreforestation.wordpress.
com/the-project

Monk Seal Foundation
www.monksealfoundation.org
Oahu: (808) 220-7802

Nature Conservancy of Hawai'i
www.nature.org/ourinitiatives/
regions/northamerica/unitedstates/
hawaii
(808) 545-2019

Outdoor Circle
www.outdoorcircle.org
(808) 593-0300

Paepae o He'eia:
Friends of He'eia Fishpond
paepaeoheeia.org

Partnership to Protect Hawai'i's
Native Species
removeratsrestorehawaii.org

Sierra Club O'ahu
www.hi.sierraclub.org/oahu
(808) 234-9779

Surfrider Foundation
oahu.surfrider.org
(808) 942-3841

Waikalua Loko Fishpond
Preservation Society
waikalualokofishpond.org
(808) 392-1284

Wild Dolphin Foundation
www.wilddolphin.org
(808) 620-6940

Photo and Illustration Credits

I would like to thank the following agencies, departments and individuals who provided images and illustrations used in this book.

Pg. 2, Hawaiian Hotspot. Tasa Graphic Arts, Inc.

Pg. 2, Pacific region tectonic plates. NPS

Pg. 3, Hawaiian Island-Emperor Seamount Chain. NOAA

Pg. 4, Kure Atoll. © Robert Shallenberger

Pg. 5, Nu'uanu landslide eastern O'ahu. Paul Johnson and SOEST.

Pg. 7, Le'ahi or Diamond Head Crater. Cecilia Walther

Pg. 9, O'ahu offshore islets. Forest & Kim Starr

Pg. 10, School of Ocean and Earth Science and Technology. Paul Johnson and SOEST.

Pg. 12, Orographic Effect. University of Hawai'i Geography Department

Pg. 12, Rainfall Map. University of Hawai'i Geography Department

Pg. 13, 4.25-inch hailstone that dropped during a supercell thunderstorm in 2012. NOAA

Pg. 14, Flood damage in Mānoa Valley, October 30, 2004. NOAA

Pg. 15, Hurricane 'Iniki. NOAA

Pg. 17, Damage to road in southeast O'ahu from April 1, 1946 tsunami. NOAA/NGDC, Orville T. Magoon

Pg. 19, © Martine Oger|Dreamstime.com

Pg. 20, 'Ōpe'ape'a or Hawaiian hoary bat *(Lasiurus cinereus semotus)*. USGS/Frank Bonaccorso

Pg. 23, Native O'ahu tree snails. Wikipedia Commons

Pg. 26, O'ahu Moa Nalo painting. Julian Hume

Pg. 26, 'Iole or Polynesian rat *(Rattus exulans)*. Wikipedia Commons

Pg. 28, King George and the Queen Charlotte of Koko Head, 1786. Raymond Massey. www.masseymarineart.com

Pg. 29, Moho or Hawaiian Rail *(Porzana sandwichensis)*. Wikipedia Commons / Frederick Frohawk

Pg. 32, Illustration of protected areas on O'ahu. TNC Hawai'i

Pg. 46, Brown tree snake *(Boiga irregularis)*. Wikipedia Commons

Pg. 51, Kamehameha butterfly *(Vanessa tameamea)*. Forest & Kim Starr

Pg. 51, Blackburn's little blue butterfly *(Udara blackburni)*. Forest & Kim Starr

Pg. 55, Extinct O'ahu forest birds: 'Ō'ō *(moho apicalis)*,' O'ū *(Psittirostra psittacea)*, the Greater 'Akialoa *(Akialoa ellisiana ellisiana)*, the Nuku pu'u *(Hemignathus lucidus)*. Julian Hume

Pg. 56, O'ahu 'Alauahio or O'ahu Creeper *(Paroreomyza maculata)*. Wikipedia Commons/John Gerrard Keulemans

Pg. 88, "Kings Highway," an old stone road built sometime after 1825. Hawai'i State Archives

LIST OF ABBREVIATIONS
USGS- United States Geological Survey
NPS- National Park Service
NOAA- National Oceanic and Atmospheric Administration
USF&W- United States Fish and Wildlife Service
HIDOT- Hawai'i Department of Transportation
TNC Hawai'i- The Nature Conservancy of Hawai'i
DOFAW- Hawai'i Department of Forestry and Wildlife

Glossary

Adaptive radiation: A process in which organisms diversify rapidly into a multitude of new forms, particularly when a change in the environment makes new resources available, creates new challenges, and opens environmental niches.

Alien: Animals, plants, or other organisms introduced by man into places out of their natural range of distribution, where they become established and disperse, generating a negative impact on the local ecosystem and species.

Aquifer: An underground layer of water-bearing permeable rock or unconsolidated materials (gravel, sand, or silt) from which groundwater can be extracted using a water well.

Archipelago: A collection of islands, sometimes called an island group or island chain.

Chemical defense in plants: Many plants produce chemicals that change the behavior, growth, or survival of herbivores. These chemical defenses can act as repellents or toxins to herbivores or reduce plant digestibility. Some plants encourage the presence of natural enemies of herbivores, which in turn protect the plant.

Cinder cone: A steep conical hill of tephra (volcanic debris) that accumulates around and downwind from a volcanic eruption.

Coevolution: The change of a biological object triggered by the change of a related object.

Deforestation: The conversion of forested areas to nonforest land use. It can be the result of the deliberate removal of forest cover for agriculture or urban development, or it can be a consequence of grazing animals, wild or domesticated.

Divergence: The evolutionary tendency or process by which animals or plants that are descended from a common ancestor evolve into different forms when living under different conditions.

Ecological: Relating to or concerned with the relation of living organisms to one another and to their physical surroundings.

Ecological niche: A term describing the relational position of a species or population in an ecosystem.

Ecosystem: The community of living organisms in a particular place, together with the nonliving physical environment in which they live.

Endemic: Confined to a particular geographic area and with a specific distribution; found nowhere else.

Evolution: The process by which different kinds of living organisms are thought to have developed and diversified from earlier forms during the history of the Earth. Consists of changes in the heritable traits of a population of organisms as successive generations replace one another. It is populations of organisms that evolve, not individual organisms.

Extant: A term commonly in use in biology to refer to taxa (singular, taxon), such as species, genera, and families, that are still in existence, meaning *still alive* as opposed to *extinct*.

Fauna: All of the animal life of any particular region or time.

Flora: The plant life occurring in a particular region or time, generally the naturally occurring or indigenous native plant life.

Herbivore: An animal anatomically and physiologically adapted to eating plant material, such as foliage, for the main component of its diet. As a result of their plant diet, herbivorous animals typically have mouthparts adapted to rasping or grinding.

Infestation: To overrun in large numbers, usually so as to be harmful.

Invasive species: Introduced species (also called nonindigenous or nonnative) that adversely affect the habitats and bioregions they invade economically, environmentally, and/or ecologically.

Jet stream: A high-speed, meandering wind current, generally moving from a westerly direction at speeds often exceeding 250 miles per hour at altitudes of 6 to 9 miles.

Life zone: A geographic region or area defined by its characteristic life forms.

Microorganism: Any organism too small to be viewed by the unaided eye, as bacteria, protozoa, and some fungi and algae.

Native: An organism that originated in the area in which it lives.

Naturalized: Thoroughly established and replacing itself by vegetative or sexual means but originally coming from another area. As used here, introduced—intentionally or unintentionally—by man or his activities.

Organism: Any contiguous living system, such as an animal, insect, plant, or bacterium. All known types of organisms are capable of some degree of response to stimuli, reproduction, growth and development, and self-regulation.

Orinthophilous: Pollinated by birds.

Pest: Any animal, plant, or disease that is injurious to agriculture, commerce, human health, or the environment.

Plant community: A collection of plant species within a designated geographical unit that forms a relatively uniform patch, distinguishable from neighboring patches of different vegetation types. The components of each plant community are influenced by soil type, topography, climate, and human disturbance.

Pollinator: The biotic agent (vector) that moves pollen from the male anthers of a flower to the female stigma of a flower to accomplish fertilization.

Propagule: Any material that is used for the purpose of propagating an organism to the next stage in its life cycle via dispersal. The propagule is usually distinct in form from the parent organism. Propagules are produced by plants (in the form of seeds or spores), fungi (in the form of spores), and bacteria.

Seed: An embryonic plant enclosed in a protective outer covering called the seed coat, usually with some stored food.

Spore: A unit of asexual reproduction that may be adapted for dispersal and for survival, often for extended periods of time, in unfavorable conditions.

Subfossil: A term applied to the remains of a once-living organism in cases where the remains are not considered to be fully fossil for one of two possible reasons: either that not enough time has elapsed since the animal died, or that the conditions in which the remains were deposited were not optimal for fossilization.

Tuff cone: A cone formed by magma-water eruptions. They have steep sides and crater floors that lie above ground level.

Vagrant: A phenomenon in biology whereby individual animals appear well outside their normal range.

Watershed: The area of land where all of the water that is under it or drains off of it goes into the same place.

Weed: A plant that aggressively colonizes disturbed habitats or places where it is not desired.

Index

'Ua'u Kani, 94